3/1/2020

D1603837

Praise for *More Precious than Diamonds*

Life can be difficult as we struggle with our self-worth. Darlene Sala's *More Precious than Diamonds* will make you pause, reflect, and pray as you read. She helps us understand how deep the Father's love for us is, how precious we are in His sight . . . and how His love carries us to live out His wonderful plan and purpose for our lives. So moving—so real!

– Coney Reyes
Multi-awarded actress, TV host and producer

This masterpiece is written by a God-inspired writer for all women who are depressed, angry, and who feel helpless and worthless. After reading this book, I now know my true value and am comforted, assured, and filled with hope, knowing that I have a God who cares and is in charge. Darlene Sala uses true-to-life stories and biblical passages to illustrate this clearly. *More Precious than Diamonds* is a must-read book for all women—if possible, read repeatedly.

– Joan Tan Garcia, MD
Past President, Phil. Society of Climacteric Medicine and Phil. Society of Reproductive Endocrinology & Infertility

Written from the heart of a woman who has intimately walked with God for many years, this refreshing book will open the eyes of the heart of every woman who reads it —to see how precious and extremely valued she is in the eyes of her Creator, who uniquely shaped her to make a difference in this world.

– Deonna Tan-Chi
International speaker and Bible teacher
Wife of Senior Pastor Peter Tan-Chi, Christ's Commission Fellowship, Pasig, Metro Manila

In my younger years, I felt ugly and unpopular among my peers. When I grew up and got married, I made mistakes and my marriage experienced failures. When my daughter Clarissa was born with Down syndrome, I questioned God, "Why me?" Darlene's book is a reminder to me that although we are all diamonds in the rough, God can cut our flaws, and turn our failures into victories, our mourning into dancing, and our ashes into beauty. As I read her book, I heard God say, "Malu, you are more precious to Me than diamonds. Your husband and your daughter are My tools to cut and polish you."

– Malu Tiongson-Ortiz
Author of *Embracing God's Purpose for My Child with Special Needs* and *Ikaw Na Ang Maganda*

Women, like men, search for security and significance in life, thinking that beauty, background, social status, or net worth could be the answer—but this is all in vain. The good news is that only through the redemption of Jesus Christ will we find our inherent self-worth and lasting joy.

Using real stories, Scripture teachings, and life experiences and encounters, Darlene Sala reminds us in this important and excellent book to look inside ourselves—to appreciate who we are in Christ. In wonder and gratitude, we should not waste our lives away working for diamonds or seeking someone who can buy us diamonds to feel good. *We are the diamonds.*

– Grace Shangkuan-Koo, PhD
Associate Professor of Educational Psychology at the University of the Philippines
Author of *Raising Wise Dads, Moms, and Kids; Guarding Your Heart and Mind: A Guide to Spiritual and Psychological Well-Being*
Christian psychologist

In *More Precious than Diamonds*, Darlene Sala gives you a glimpse into the interesting world of diamonds, insightfully explaining the parallelism between diamond cutting and the refinement that God performs in us. Deep biblical principles are articulated in a manner that makes them easy to understand. Through this book, you will be truly grateful for how God values your uniqueness, deeply encouraged because He secures your worth in Him, and excited to shine for His glory because to Him, you are indeed more precious than diamonds!

– Aileen Espinosa Cura
Classical performing artist/vocal soloist
Wife of Dan Cura, President of the Far East Broadcasting Company (FEBC), Philippines

"Does this world really need me? How valuable am I?" Women of all ages, single or married, go through an identity crisis at some point in their lives. How wonderful to know, as Darlene Sala vividly describes it, that we are "more precious than diamonds."

Darlene says, "He has formed many diamonds, but He made only one *you*! . . . He made you because He wants someone exactly like you." Discover more about your value and the precious God who loves you through this gem of a book.

– Marie A. Bonifacio
Writer, artist, speaker
Wife of Senior Pastor Joey Bonifacio, Victory Christian Fellowship, Taguig City, Metro Manila

A must-have for all women! This book has ministered to me immensely! As a woman juggling theater and Christian ministry, I have just entered my 40s and have been jolted many times by new issues I was not prepared for. Darlene Sala relates in a real and encouraging way to issues we women face. She lovingly brings us back to Jesus, in whom we find our real value and worth. This book is a timeless and powerful help for women of all ages as we combat and win over our self-image and identity struggles. This book affirms that to our Creator, we are indeed more precious than diamonds!

– Mayen Bustamante-Cadd
Theater artist and teacher
Acting coach, Sword Productions, Makati City, Metro Manila

MORE PRECIOUS THAN
DIAMONDS

*Biblical Meditations
on a Woman's Worth in God's Eyes*

Darlene Sala

OMF LITERATURE INC.

Manila, Philippines

More Precious than Diamonds

Biblical Meditations on a Woman's Worth in God's Eyes
Copyright © 2015 by Darlene Sala

Published in the Philippines (2015) by
OMF Literature, Inc.
*776 Boni Avenue
Mandaluyong City, Metro Manila
www.omflit.com*

*Cover design by Amor Aurelio Alvarez
Page design by Aileen Barrongo*

ISBN 978-971-009-426-4

Printed in the Philippines

To every woman
who has ever doubted her own worth.
Or doesn't know where to go from where she is.
Or is losing heart.

May God help you to see yourself
as the precious gem that you are—
valuable to God and others,
created to be cherished and protected,
in a setting where your life will sparkle
for God's eternal purpose.

Contents

Introduction

You've read the title of this book. But is it true for you? I mean, does God *really* think you are more precious than diamonds?

It's so easy to make an assertion without facts to back it up. You could have read the title, stopped there, assumed it is true, then gone away feeling better about yourself without having any foundation on which to base your good feelings. And how long would that last? Not very long, I'm afraid.

What you and I need is not merely to feel good about ourselves. We need to know the *truth* about ourselves. In my book *Created for a Purpose* I quote Stephen Arterburn, Chairman and CEO of New Life Treatment Centers, who said that the goal of secular counseling is to make you feel *good* about yourself, but the goal of Biblical counseling is to make you feel *right* about yourself.

God is not interested in you and me merely feeling good about ourselves. He wants us to feel right about ourselves. That's why He has given us the Bible, His Word, where we learn that we truly are more precious to Him than diamonds—or rubies or gold.

You may be feeling pretty worthless right now, beaten down. Life has thrown more at you than you can handle. You don't feel you are worth a rhinestone, let alone a diamond. Take heart. "You are precious and honored in my sight," says God, "and . . . I love you" (Isaiah 43:4). Don't *feel* it? Read on . . .

PART ONE

You are Valuable

PRE·CIOUS (adjective): of great value; too important to be wasted or treated carelessly

Synonyms: valuable, costly, expensive, priceless, highly esteemed, cherished, of great value, treasured, prized, dearest, beloved

A Diamond is Forever—
and So Are You

Frances Gerety was exhausted. The young copy-writer had been hired in 1943 to add a "woman's touch" to the De Beers diamond advertising campaign for her employer, Philadelphia ad agency N.W. Ayer & Son. Frances had just finished a series of ads one evening and was headed for bed, when she suddenly realized she had forgotten to create a signature line for the ads. Exhausted, she said, "Dear God, send me a line," scribbled something on a slip of paper, and went to sleep.

Now, marketing diamonds had been a big part of the success of the De Beers company, that, since the 1800s until recent years, had dominated the entire diamond industry. When Frances looked at her note the next morning, she saw she had written, "A Diamond Is Forever." Not overly impressed, she nevertheless presented the slogan at a company meeting. As they say, the rest is history.

"A Diamond Is Forever" has appeared in every De Beers engagement ad since 1948, and for the next twenty-five years, Frances Gerety wrote all of the company's ads. In 1999, two weeks before Ms. Gerety died at the age of eighty-three, *Advertising Age* magazine named "A Diamond Is Forever" the slogan of the century.[1]

But, you are forever, too! God came up with the idea long before an ad copywriter wrote her slogan. His plan has always been for us to be with Him for all eternity—forever.

When I was looking for verses in the Bible that tell us we have eternal life if we believe in Jesus, I was impressed by the fact that the Apostle John had written most of them. The truth of us living forever with the Lord must have touched his heart in a special way, for he is the one who recorded all of these words of Jesus (emphasis mine):

> ". . . everyone who believes may have *eternal life* in him." *(John 3:15)*

"Very truly I tell you, whoever hears my word and believes him who sent me has *eternal life* and will not be judged but has crossed over from death to life." *(John 5:24)*

"My sheep listen to my voice; I know them, and they follow me. I give them *eternal life*, and they shall never perish; no one will snatch them out of my hand." *(John 10:27–28)*

"Now this is *eternal life*: that they know you, the only true God, and Jesus Christ, whom you have sent." *(John 17:3)*

"For my Father's will is that everyone who looks to the Son and believes in him shall have *eternal life*, and I will raise them up at the last day." *(John 6:40)*

John gave us his reason for writing these truths: "I write these things to you who believe in the name of the Son of God so that you may *know* that you have eternal life" (1 John 5:13).

Take a close look at that last statement of John's. See that word *know*? John didn't want you to have any doubt about your future.

He didn't say that you can merely *hope* that you have eternal life. No, you can *know*! Don't ever let Satan cheat you out of that confidence. Your assurance is not dependent on your being sinless. It's fully based on Jesus' sacrifice for you. You are so very precious to Him, and when you put your faith in Him, your future is as certain as the promises of God—forever!

Cry from my Heart

Thank You that I can know beyond the shadow of a doubt that I have eternal life. Thank You that You want me with You forever.

Diamonds—
Worth How Much?

Now, since you are more precious than diamonds, you need to know your comparative value.

You are worth well more than . . . $39 million! That's how much a single diamond, bought at auction in New York City on April 9, 2013, cost. This rare 34.65-carat pink gem, nicknamed the Princie Diamond, was sold to an anonymous collector for what was at that time the second highest price ever paid for a diamond.

No, it's not the most costly diamond ever sold, but the story behind it is fascinating. Discovered more than three hundred years ago in India, the diamond first belonged to the Nizams, the royal family of Hyderabad, whose emperors were direct descendants of Genghis

Khan and owned and ruled a section of India from 1526 to 1948. On this land were located the Golconda mines—at that time the only known diamond mines in the world—and this is where the Princie Diamond was discovered.[2]

I had never even heard of Hyderabad—until several years ago when I was sorting some memorabilia stored in a closet. There, on the back of a newspaper obituary of my great-grandmother, of all places, I found an undated article that said the "Nizam of Hyderabad is by far the wealthiest man on earth . . . worth at least one billion dollars. His riches cannot be computed."

The old newspaper clipping went on to say that the Nizam had eight hundred tons of gold stored up in a strong room, and that he had so many diamonds, rubies, emeralds, and pearls that he could use *shovels* to take them from the bins where they were stored. The *New York Times* reported that he owned enough pearls to fill an Olympic-sized swimming pool![3]

Calculating the Nizam's modern-day worth, accounting for inflation, today he would be worth about $236 billion.[4] By contrast, Bill Gates, who in 2014 was declared the richest man in the world, is worth $76 billion.[5]

I was curious to know more.

Of the seven successive rulers, or Nizams, of Hyderabad, Mir Osman Ali Khan was the wealthiest, ruling from 1911 to 1948. He had at least twelve palaces, and his main palace had six thousand staffers. The only job thirty-eight of them were entrusted with was dusting chandeliers. The world's richest man was an enigma—so penny-pinching that he wore the same fez cap for thirty-five years, wore crumpled pajamas, ate off a tin plate, and smoked cigarette butts, refusing to buy even one fresh pack all his life. He also had a habit of hoarding cash, that once led rats to chew their way through three million pounds in British banknotes in a palace basement.[6]

So where did he get his astounding wealth? Diamonds! The royal family not only owned the Golconda mines but traded in diamonds as well. For example, the Nizam's father obtained the famous Jacob Diamond—four hundred carats and the world's fifth largest. The value of the Jacob Diamond alone (now owned by the government of India) is $4 billion. You'd think a special safe would have been constructed to protect such an amazing stone. But the fact is that the seventh Nizam found the duck-egg-sized diamond hidden in his father's slippers and used it as a paperweight until he realized its value.[7]

Did the Nizam's incredible wealth in diamonds bring happiness to his family? Not exactly. Before the Nizam died in 1967, he had sired children from eighty-six mistresses in his harem and had more than a hundred illegitimate children.[8] He left his estate to his grandson, though the Indian government claimed much of it in back taxes. By the 1990s, claimants to his wealth had gone up to four hundred legal heirs. Grandson Mukarram Jah so despised the rancor and hostility that ensued over the remaining wealth that he moved to Australia, choosing to run a tractor as a gentleman farmer on a sheep ranch. And after five marriages and divorces, including one to Miss Turkey, the last we know, he was living alone in a two-room bare-wall apartment in Turkey. Obviously, diamonds are no guarantee of happiness!

Curious about the highest price ever paid for a diamond? For a long time, $45 million was the record.

But on November 13, 2013, a 59.6-carat flawless pink diamond called the "Pink Star" was auctioned by Sotheby's for a whopping $83.2 million. *Cha-ching!* That made it the most expensive jewel or diamond ever sold at auction.[9]

The largest diamond ever discovered, the Cullinan, weighed 3,106 carats (that's about one and a third pounds) in its rough form. You'll read its story in a few more pages. The most precious diamond, however, based on its importance and value, is the Koh-i-noor, now part of the British Crown Jewels collection. According to experts, the gem, which originated in Hyderabad, cannot be valued. It is calculated to be approximately 3.5 times the wealth of the whole world.[10]

How on earth did the world ever get these amazing jewels in the first place? Henry Kissinger, the American statesman, is credited with saying that a diamond is just a piece of charcoal that handled stress exceptionally well. In a sense, that is very true, for diamonds are pieces of carbon formed about a hundred miles below the surface of the earth in the part that is very hot, where the weight of the overlying rock, combined with the heat and high pressure, allow the diamond crystals to grow. Each one-carat diamond represents "literally billions and billions of carbon crystals that all had to lock into place to form this very orderly crystalline structure"—the hardest naturally occurring mineral in the world.[11]

What makes diamonds so expensive is the process needed to turn them from rough stones into gems that can be made into jewelry. Only about 20 percent of diamonds make the grade. The others, because of their hardness, are used in industry or ground into boart—diamond dust used to cut and polish gemstone diamonds. The cutting and polishing, of course, require great skill. The end result is something of great beauty, great individuality . . . and great worth.

Cry from my Heart | *Lord, I don't feel worth anything like an $83 million diamond. Help me to accept my worth in Your sight.*

More Precious than Diamonds

God has lots of diamonds. I think He must smile as He sees human beings working the ground and even the bottom of the ocean, searching for them. He knows exactly where they are.

But diamonds just aren't that precious to God. Nor are other costly stones—or even gold. After all, in heaven He uses gold for paving streets and pearls for gates (Revelation 21:21). And He uses gems to decorate the foundations of the heavenly city (verse 19).

But you? That's another matter. He has formed many diamonds, but He made only one *you*. You are unique. You are unlike anyone else who has ever lived or ever will live. He made you because He wants someone exactly like you.

Oh yes, like diamonds, we're flawed. That's one way gemologists identify them—by the unique flaws or inclusions they find in them. But God came up with an extravagant plan to solve that problem of our flaws—a solution that cost God the very life of His Son when He died in our place on the cross. The cross is the center-piece of God's display of His love for us.

Think about this. We are so precious to God that He sent His only Son, Jesus, to this earth to die so you and I wouldn't have to die for the sins we've committed. David Eckman pictures God explaining this to us:

> "My Son is dying for you because you
> are worth a Son to Me."[12]

Just think of it—*"you are worth a Son to Me."*

I think it's very sad that today we don't hear that message as clearly as we should. Much religious teaching is directed at merely making me feel good about myself. TV personality Larry King once asked the pastor of a mega-church why he didn't have a cross anywhere in his church. "We believe in the cross, but the cross reminds people of pain," responded the pastor, "and we want people who come to be filled with positive thoughts." How sad, for the cross of Jesus tells us beyond the shadow of a doubt of our worth in God's sight.

What *is* precious to God is *you* and *me*—living to glorify Him. We'll look at that thought in more depth later in this book.

When we place our faith in Jesus as our Savior, He comes to live within us in the person of the Holy Spirit. The Apostle Paul said, "I have been crucified with Christ and I no longer live, but Christ lives in me" (Galatians 2:20). Then in 2 Corinthians 4:7, he explains that ". . . we have this treasure in jars of clay to show that this all-surpassing power is from God and not from us." To put it simply, God lives in our "clay pots."

In Bible days people used clay pots to hold necessities like water and grain. But today we don't use clay pots very much. We use plastic instead, such as for paint and detergent. Have you noticed how hard it is to throw away one of these buckets? We keep them, thinking they'll be handy for future use—and so they stack up in our homes.

How much is a used plastic bucket worth? Probably less than a dollar. But let's say your grandmother left you her two-carat diamond necklace when she died, and now you're going on a trip lasting several weeks. You don't want to leave the necklace in your jewelry box for fear it would be stolen while you're gone, so you try to think of a place where a thief wouldn't think of looking. And so you decide to bury it deep in that plastic bucket of detergent near your washing machine.

Hey, how much is that bucket worth *now*? A great deal! It's what is *in* the bucket that makes it so valuable. When we put our faith in Jesus Christ, He chooses to take up residence in our hearts. We are extremely valuable—precious—to Him.

But we often don't *feel* valuable. That's because today's woman is repeatedly forced to compare herself with perfection. She is barraged today with more images of the perfect face and perfect body (airbrushed, of course) than at any time in human history. She is constantly bombarded on her cell phone and computer with a flow of glowing media images in filtered, living color. And let's hope your home looks like something on the Home and Garden Channel, and the dinners you're whipping up come straight from the Food Channel recipes.

Celebrities have all sorts of professional help with their appearance, but now so can you—if you can afford it! In recent years dermatology has taken its place alongside cosmetic surgery in

offering to take ten years off a woman's appearance. These days the business of plastic surgery
mushrooms as women set out on their personal
quests for self-worth, hoping that a perfect nose
makes a perfect person.

Increasingly, we self-publish the details of our
daily lives on social media. Take a look at your
posts on Facebook. When you post a picture or
a comment, you are actually writing a history
of your life, one post at a time. While doing
this may make you feel better about yourself,
another woman may be depressed from seeing
the post of you and your husband celebrating
your wedding anniversary, and think, "Celebrating? My husband and I aren't even speaking!" or
"Now that I've turned fifty, no one would want
to marry *me*."

Small business coach Alice Arenas, in an
online article entitled "Social Media Self-Esteem
—True Confessions," points out the effect of
this overexposure of our private lives in the
comments she has overheard, including these:

- I saw on Foursquare that the three of
  them had dinner. Why wasn't I invited?

- Why did so-and-so unfriend me on
  Facebook?

- No one is re-tweeting me. Am I doing something wrong?

- Yesterday I had eight hundred views on my blog. Today I have only three hundred. It's so depressing.[13]

Best-selling author Ann Voskamp writes: "I want to tell . . . every woman browsing through a fashion magazine, standing on a scale, scrolling through Pinterest, clicking through blogs, looking in a mirror: Every yardstick always becomes a billystick. Pick up a yardstick to measure your life against anyone else's and you've just picked up a stick and beaten up on your own soul."[14]

My own definition of self-worth is very simple. As a woman, I ask myself, "Am I a person of value?" If my answer is yes, I have self-worth. If my answer is no—if I truly believe I have little value in this world—my life will be a constant struggle. If we look at our worth from a human perspective, then we will *always* see something flawed and weak.

We simply can't "do it all." But when our self-worth is secure through Christ, we will be better able to leave our failures in God's hands, knowing it is His strength that is at work in our lives, not our own. God's perspective is eternal —to Him we are precious every day of our lives.

Listen to Father God saying to you, "You are worth a Son to Me. I want to have a close and intimate relationship with you." Run—yes, run to His arms today. Don't wait another minute. Let Him whisper these words to you: "I love you. I love you."

| *Cry* from my Heart | *Lord, You have lots of diamonds—but only one me! What an amazing thought! Help me not to forget how much You love me.* |

Marilyn Monroe—
and You

Born Norma Jeane Mortenson, she lived only thirty-six years. As Marilyn Monroe, she became an actress, model, and singer in the fifties and early sixties, reaching the pinnacle of fame. Marilyn Monroe is considered by many to be the quintessential American sex symbol.

But as Norma Jeane, she spent much of her childhood in foster homes because her mother was psychiatrically ill and financially unable to care for her.[15] Norma Jeane was the illegitimate daughter of Edward Mortenson, who abandoned her mother before she was born and was killed in a motorcycle accident when she was only three years old. Several offers to adopt her were rejected by her mentally ill mother. In her autobiography *My Story*, Monroe recalls her mother "screaming and laughing" as she was forcibly removed to the State Hospital in Norwalk, California. At age five, Norma Jeane was declared a ward of the state.[16] Attempts at sexual assault by several people she lived with were part of her childhood.

Eventually, though, with much hard work Marilyn Monroe became a successful model. At one point, desperately in need of money, she posed for a set of nude photographs, and later one of those pictures became the very first *Playboy* centerfold. All in all, she appeared in 29 movies with major film companies. After her death, the American Film Institute ranked her the sixth-greatest female star of all time.

One of the songs Marilyn Monroe became known for was "Diamonds Are a Girl's Best Friend," from the 1953 film "Gentlemen Prefer Blondes." One can't help thinking that the title of the song is descriptive of Marilyn's own life, since so many people, especially in her early years, had let her down.

Attracting male attention all her life, Marilyn would probably have agreed in the end that diamonds were better friends. No one knows how many relationships she had, but they included one with President John F. Kennedy and possibly one with his brother Bobby Kennedy. Three marriages—to James Dougherty, baseball legend Joe DiMaggio, and playwright Arthur Miller—ended in divorce. And although Marilyn dearly wanted children, she suffered two miscarriages and an ectopic pregnancy.

Her dependence on daily visits with her psychiatrist, along with her use of alcohol and barbiturates in the latter years of her short life, imprint her story with a profound sadness. Long after she was famous, Marilyn would go to night-clubs disguised in a black wig to see if she could still attract a man as Norma Jeane. Friends said that when Marilyn turned thirty-six, she seemed to feel she was "over the hill," aware that some-one younger and prettier would eventually take her place in the limelight.[17] That same year her life ended because of a drug overdose—whether accidental or suicidal, we'll never know. Mari-lyn Monroe had fame, beauty, talent, success, wealth—and yes, even diamonds. But her life left the taste of ashes. All her life was a quest for unlimited love, and she never found it.

Most women, whether famous or not, get their sense of value from one or more of these three areas:

- Our appearance—our beauty, our sense of style, our skill in grooming

- Our accomplishments—our intelligence, our abilities, our talents

- Our relationships—as wives, mothers, friends

There's nothing wrong with this—we all do it. But sooner or later each of these areas will undergo change. We'll eventually age. Someone will come along who is smarter or more gifted than we are. Our children will grow up and leave home. Our best friend might prefer being friends with someone else.

You need a source of esteem that will *never* change. And that ultimate source is found in what God thinks of you.

You are unique. God gave you characteristics that make you who are. Of all the people He created in the world, there is not one replica of you. And you are the person God wants a relationship with. He wants His beauty to flow through your life.

How do you know you are precious to God? Primarily because of one great reason: Jesus died for you. God's willingness to send His Son from heaven to this earth to die in our place tells us we have unbelievable value in His sight.

The Apostle John said, "Greater love has no one than this: to lay down one's life for one's friends" (John 15:13). That's what Jesus did for us—except that He went one step further. "Very rarely will anyone die for a righteous person, though for a good person someone might possibly dare to die. But God demonstrates his own love for us in this: While we were still sinners, Christ died for us" (Romans 5:7–8).

Our first parents, Adam and Eve, sinned. They chose their own way instead of God's. And through the centuries, men and women have continued to choose their own way instead of God's. "We all, like sheep, have gone astray, each of us has turned to our *own way*" (Isaiah 53:6, italics mine). That's the real meaning of sin.

Ever since Adam and Eve sinned, there has been a God-shaped emptiness in the human heart that we have tried to fill with things and people in order to find peace and happiness. It's a heart-hunger. Some of us thought that when we got married, that big hole would be filled. So we put an impossible burden on our husbands, expecting them to meet every need we'd ever have. As wonderful as marriage can be, it was never meant to replace the relationship between you and God. Children cannot fill that hole. They meet a need in the heart of women to nurture, but children cannot meet the need we have for God. Friendship cannot fill that hole either. We hunger for the Bread of Life and thirst for the Water of Life, and nothing else will fully satisfy.

Many people believe God is so kind and loving that of course, He will forgive our sins. But that is not the reason God forgives. The only way God can forgive us is because Jesus paid the price for our sin. It's the greatest love story in the world.

Here's an interesting thought for you: Mary became pregnant by the Holy Spirit with that awesome God-child. Realize that means God's Son was willing to become one cell at the moment of conception—a diploid cell—the size of the period at the end of this sentence. God's Son contained in one cell!

God loved us. And God's love compelled Him to come up with an incredible plan to save us—all because He loved us so very much. "This is real love—not that we loved God, but that he loved us and sent his Son as a sacrifice to take away our sins" (1 John 4:10 NLT). Yes, you and I deserve to die for our sins, but Jesus died in our place. Incredible, unbelievable love!

When I think about the price Christ paid for me, I ask myself, *Am I worth it?* I don't think so, but He does, and that's all that matters. My value is not dependent upon any goodness in me, praise God! He does not love you and me because we are good. He does not love us because we are talented, or beautiful, or even unselfish and generous. He simply loves us unconditionally.

If you do not have a personal relationship with Jesus Christ, this is the perfect time to give your life to Him. If you have never responded to His love and asked Him to forgive your sins and be your Savior and Lord, do it now—before you close this book. There is no better time. You can meet Jesus, and He will become very real to you. He waits to fill the empty place in your heart.

Cry from my Heart

Thank You, thank You for the price You paid to have a relationship with me. Your love is amazing!

For When You Want to Freak Out because You Just Keep Getting Older

Not only is my bra size unimpressive by worldly standards, but NOW I am getting older too. Older, wrinklier, and squishier. Great. Just fantastic.

And this—this place of deep, deep insecurity is the exact place where I have to turn to the Father for truth. Because my worth? It isn't found in any number associated with my body. Not the number on my scale. Not the number on my blue jeans. Not the number on my bra. Not the number that tells just how old this body is.

My ultimate worth is found in a different set of numbers—as in thirty-three years spent in humble earthbound service instead of on a rightful heavenly throne. It is found in three nails piercing willing hands and feet and six excruciating hours spent hanging on a cross. The numbers associated with Jesus, who said I was worth dying for, are the only numbers that count. And while the numbers associated with my body will always fluctuate, those numbers connected to Jesus will never change. My worth is secure and Rock-solid in Him.

Kimberly D. Henderson[18]

A Diamond
in the Rough

On January 25, 1905, a glint on the side of a mine pit caught the eye of Surface Manager Frederick Wells as he went about his rounds at the Premier Diamond Mining Company in Cullinan, Transvaal (now known as South Africa). He climbed down the side to investigate.

Using his penknife, Wells extracted that day what turned out to be the largest rough diamond ever found. Once he retrieved the stone, he immediately took it to the mine office, where he had to persuade his colleagues to weigh it, after one exclaimed, "This is no diamond!" and threw it out the window. The rough diamond weighed an astonishing 3,106 carats (621 grams), or more than one and one-third pounds.[19] It was so large that a man's fist could not close around it.

In a short time, the mining company sold the diamond, named "The Cullinan," to the Transvaal government so that they could present it to England's King Edward VII as a sign of gratitude for his passing the government from British rule to state rule. But how would they get such a costly stone safely across thousands of miles of ocean from South Africa to London? The government decided to send a decoy of the stone to Europe on a heavily guarded ship, while the real diamond was—can you believe it?—sent by ordinary parcel post![20]

When King Edward received the amazing gift, he commissioned the celebrated firm of I. J. Asscher of Amsterdam to cut and polish the diamond. It was both an honor and a burden, because of the high probability that the stone could be ruined.

Because of the extreme complexity of cutting diamonds, unique tools, equipment, and techniques were required, along with an artist's eye, a surgeon's skill, and specialized knowledge of the makeup of the stones. When Joseph Asscher made that first critical cut on the Cullinan, he did not have the benefit of today's technology that is now used to turn rough diamonds into gemstones. In our time, scanning devices are used to get a three-dimensional computer model of the rough stone. Flaws are photographed and placed on the 3D model, which is then used to find an optimal way to cut the stone.[21] Joseph did not have these tools to help him.

A painstaking eight months of work began. To accommodate such a large diamond, the company had to build all-new, larger equipment, such as a polishing wheel twice the size normally used. The tension was extremely high. As he worked on the diamond, Asscher's bosses were constantly watching him.[22]

For days Joseph Asscher did nothing but analyze the stone to find the natural cleavage where he could make the breaks. Then on February 10, 1908, he finally started cutting. It took four days for him to scratch a half-inch groove in the diamond with another diamond so that he could "cleave" or chop it at the point of a natural cleavage. He placed a blade in the groove and gave it a tap. Nothing happened. He did it again, and the diamond split—and it is reported that Asscher promptly fainted. If he had done it wrong, the largest diamond in the world would have shattered.

Sometimes God, too, allows cleaving in our lives that leaves us breathless. The death of a dream when the doctor reveals irreversible infertility. The revelation that a spouse has been unfaithful . . . and that it's been going on for decades. Cancer. A senseless act of violence in a school, or abuse at the hands of those who should have protected and cherished.

As Mrs. Charles Cowman wrote in her famous devotional *Streams in the Desert,*

> [God] is the most skilled lapidary in the universe. . . . As you lie in His hand now He knows just how to deal with you. Not a blow will be permitted to fall upon your shrinking soul but that the love of God permits it, and works out from its depths, blessing and spiritual enrichment unseen and unthought of by you.[23]

After the initial cut, the Cullinan was cut once more, making three pieces, then cut into nine almost-flawless stones. The resulting pieces were cut, ground, and polished by three polishers working fourteen-hour days. The end product was nine principal numbered stones (Cullinan I-IX), ninety-six small brilliants, and nine carats of unpolished fragments.[24] The largest gem, over 530 carats, is pear-shaped and was named

Cullinan 1, or the Great Star of Africa, and can be found mounted in the head of the British Sceptre with the Cross. The second largest piece, the Lesser Star of Africa, is cushion-shaped and forms part of the Imperial State Crown. Both pieces can be seen in the British Crown Jewels in the Tower of London,[25] but they bear no resemblance to the original stone.

When the Cullinan diamond was first removed from the mine, it was referred to as a "rough diamond." Most of us know people who are "diamonds in the rough." The truth is that we are all diamonds in the rough. Only God can see the stunning, multidimensional beauty that lies within us. But don't forget that God also loves us in our original condition—exactly as we are. He doesn't wait until we have had the rough places removed or until we are beautiful to regard us as valuable to Him. That said, neither does He leave us in our rough state; but He constantly shapes us so that the loveliness within is revealed. The famous British preacher Charles Spurgeon wrote, "The uncut diamond has little brilliance . . . and the untried believer is of little use or beauty."[26] God cares too much about us to let us stay like we are. I'm so thankful that when God allows painful events in my life to shape me into what He designed me to be, I have the assurance He is the Master Diamond Cutter and knows what He is doing.

Karin's story

Karin was born into a Christian family and married a man who had come to know Christ in a believing family. Then they had a baby girl. Sounds idyllic, doesn't it? But Karin and her husband, David, were not prepared for the devastating news that the child they had longed for had Down syndrome. Questions deluged their minds: "Why? What could we have done to deserve this?"

Their daughter Karissa is now in her twenties, and their question has been wonderfully transformed to "How could God possibly have thought us worthy of raising this beautiful daughter?" Gone is the resentment and pain. Because Karin and David know that the divorce rate among parents of a disabled child is 85 percent by the time the child reaches age three, they overflow with thankfulness to the Lord for bringing healing to their hearts.

But what cutting and polishing process did they go through to reach this change of heart? It certainly did not happen overnight. First there was the initial shock. Still reeling from the news, they determined to get all the information they could about their daughter's needs. They enrolled her in the very best program for children with Down syndrome and got the very best training they could for themselves.

Then with Karin's second pregnancy four years later came the great fear that this child might also have genetic abnormalities. When Evan was born a perfectly typical child, somewhat strangely, new stress entered their lives as the contrast between the development of the two children made Karissa's condition seem even more significant. Problems sprouted in their marriage. David became immersed in his career, and Karin grew increasingly concerned about Karissa's disability.

Determined not to let these issues tear them apart, Karin and David, with tears, much prayer, and much Bible study, sought counsel and worked through the issues, and God brought healing to their relationship. By the time their third child was born, they named her Hannah ("God answers") and called her their "celebration child," rejoicing that God does answer prayer and had brought restoration to their marriage.

Now they find numerous opportunities to reach out to other hurting parents and bless them with their faith and experience. Finding a dearth of fellowship opportunities for young adults with disabilities, they have collaborated with Young Life to launch a local group that would meet this need. They also counsel newly diagnosed families, sharing their story and their faith.[27]

The Master Diamond Cutter's cleaving and polishing has brought marvelous beauty and blessing to these two diamonds in the rough. Their lives now sparkle with the joy that God has given them through difficult times.

Bernadette's story

Not everyone, though, has such an inspiring conclusion to their story. For some, the cutting and polishing process continues.

Bernadette was not a believer when she met Alex. Alex professed to be a believer but was not living like one at the time. Yes, he took Bernadette to church, but God didn't rank high in his life. That all changed, however, when Alex discovered that he had leukemia. Suddenly God was a priority! The usual chemotherapy followed until Alex was finally in remission.

Unfortunately, after the crisis was over, Alex didn't think he needed God anymore and went back to his old life of barhopping and partying. But God wasn't finished with him. When once again the leukemia reared its ugly head, this time a bone marrow transplant was necessary. Alex had two days in which to have sperm frozen in case he ever wanted to father a child.

In the meantime, on her own, Bernadette had begun to explore a relationship with Christ and soon invited Him to be Lord of her life. She and Alex later married, but were unable to carry babies to full term—even with in vitro fertilization. Not long ago, though, she finally successfully conceived—what joy! At last, it seemed that her life would sparkle.

But then the dreadful news—her husband's cancer had returned; this time, the leukemic cells were concentrated in his eyelid. I wish I could tell you that the battle is over, and Bernadette and Alex are living "happily ever after." But it's an ongoing struggle for them. As Bernadette goes through the months of her pregnancy, her husband is undergoing treatment for the cancer. Friends say Bernadette's attitude is incredible as she and her husband submit to the cutting and polishing of the Master Diamond Cutter.

"God is sovereign," says Bernadette. "I want to grow through this and be an example to other believers." God is walking the painful road with them, and they are finding His strength day by day.[28]

❂ ❂ ❂

Like the diamond cutter, God uses a wide variety of methods to shape us into what He created us to be. When a diamond cutter wants to make a gem more round-shaped, he uses a procedure called "bruiting." This is the process "whereby two diamonds are set onto spinning axles turning in opposite directions, which are then set to grind against each other to shape each diamond into a round shape."[29] Eventually the cutter achieves the shape he envisioned. God sometimes uses other people to smooth the rough places off our lives, too. One friend of mine refers to her husband and children as "God's tool belt" in her life. She says that each person, along with his or her unique personality, strengths, and weaknesses, is handpicked by God to spin along (yes, sometimes in opposite directions) and rub in just the right way to perfectly "bruit" her personality into the shape it was always meant to be.

That infuriating neighbor who keeps your son's basketball when it goes over the wall into his yard. The boss who regularly gives you last-minute work just when you're about to leave the office. Or the people next door who sing karaoke until the wee hours of the morning. Irritating, isn't it! Yet, God often uses others to test our patience to show us how little it takes for us to lose the sense of His presence in our lives and to react in anger. How we need the Holy Spirit to help us when God allows "bruiting" in our lives! We should remember, though, that in all things God works for our good (Roman 8:28).

After cleaving or sawing the stone, the diamond worker then begins to make the rough diamond even more valuable by cutting, the process whereby facets are formed on the diamond. How many facets are cut depends on the future use of the diamond. Will the gem be used in jewelry or as a display item? Will it be viewed from the top or the sides? Even more basic, what is the natural type of the crystal? For the cut should take advantage of the innate shape. The round *brilliant* is the most popular cut given to a diamond; this stone is usually given 57 or 58 facets. The princess cut may have as many as 144 facets. That's a lot of cutting on a small stone!

God knows what He's doing in my life and yours. He knows our basic "shape." He knows precisely how much cutting and polishing we need in order for our lives to sparkle for Him.

Until I did some research on the subject, I had no idea how scientific the cutting of diamonds has become. I learned that scientists have developed calculations that maximize the brilliance and fire of a diamond. They refer to "computation of the three-dimensional nature of light behavior" inside a diamond, and the fact that a diamond's appearance is composed of "many light paths that reflect considerably more than two times within that diamond."[30] While those terms mean nothing to me, to a diamond cutter they mean the difference between a stone being worth hundreds of dollars or tens of thousands of dollars, depending on the cutter's knowledge and skill.

If a diamond cutter takes all these matters into consideration before he begins, dear sister, please know that God does no less for you when He begins the process of shaping and cutting in your life. He knows how He created you. He has plans for what you are to become. And He knows the best way you will show off

His workmanship. When He does any cutting in your life, you can be sure that the Master Diamond Cutter does perfect work, turning you into the beautiful jewel He created you to be. Though cutting may be painful, He makes no mistakes.

The final step in creating a gem from a rough diamond is the polishing. This process improves the smoothness of the diamond's facets. With poor polishing, the surface of a facet can be dulled. The stone may constantly look like it needs to be cleaned.

Since the diamond is the hardest known natural substance, diamond dust is about the only substance that can be applied successfully to the grinding wheel used to cut and polish the stone. Thomas Carlyle, who lost his faith during his college years but still did continue to believe there is a God, once said, "Adversity is the diamond dust heaven polishes its jewels with."[31]

One man who learned this by experience is Wang Ming-Dao, considered the father of the house church movement in China. His refusal in the 1950s to join the Three-Self Patriotic Movement resulted in his spending twenty-two years in prison. His wife was incarcerated for twenty years, and they saw each other only twice during that period. Wang endured solitary confinement, torture, and the anguish of months of meetings attempting to force confessions from him.

Wang Ming-Dao authored a little book called *A Stone Made Smooth*, obviously referring to the abrasion of trials that smooth the rough places of our lives and make us more like Christ. After his release, during one of our visits with him in Shanghai, my husband, Harold, said to him, "Brother Wang, many years ago I read your book *A Stone Made Smooth*." With a twinkle in his eye, Wang Ming-Dao responded, "Stone still not yet smooth!" He explained that God was still continuing to use the circumstances of living in a broken world to make him more Christ-like.

Our reaction to all of this cutting, grinding, and polishing may be another story. Many times I have simply wanted to say, "NO. No more. Sparkle isn't all that it's cracked up to be!" I am not alone. In 1664 a fifteen-year-old French-woman by the name of Jeanne Guyon was forced into an arranged marriage with a wealthy 38-year-old man. Ill-treated by her mother-in-law, she endured the deaths of her half sister, her mother, her son, her father, and her daughter in the first eight years of the difficult marriage. Jeanne would later come to write on God's perfect plan and blessing in suffering:

> Oh, it is true that when your Lord actually began burning, destroying, and purifying, you did not recognize that it was the hand of the Lord in your life. You certainly did not recognize the operation as something good. You had the very opposite impression! Instead, you saw all that beautiful gold in you turning black in the fire rather than becoming bright as you had expected. You stood looking at the circumstances around you that were producing all that tragedy in your life. . . . If, at that moment, the Lord had come and asked you for your active consent, at best you would hardly have been able to give it. . . . There is something you can do at times like those, however. You can remain firm in a passive consent, enduring as patiently as you can all that God has introduced into your life.[32]

There is deep peace in the quietness of surrender, as Jeanne Guyon described it.

Nearly all diamonds have flaws or inclusions, but there are some diamonds that show no flaws, and those diamonds are very, very valuable. Do you realize that's exactly how God sees you when Jesus forgives your sins and you start all over as a new creation (2 Corinthians 5:17)? Your past is wiped clean, sins forgiven and forgotten. You are a flawless gem in God's sight. When God looks at you, He does not see flaws. He sees the reflection of His Son. He promises He "remembers your sins no more" (Isaiah 43:25). And He never goes back on a promise.

When the sin of another has spilled over into your life, you are still a flawless gem in God's sight. You may feel that you have been used up, violated, broken irrevocably, never to sparkle again. The polishing you require may be undertaken with incomparable tenderness and gentleness. Your soul may require the healing salve of a Savior who had the utmost compassion for women in any state in which He encountered them. Regardless of the past, our future as God's precious jewels is very bright.

When a diamond cutter is finished, the gem shows its previously unseen eye-catching brilliance and beauty. In our case, that's a process that continues throughout our lives as the Master shapes us, until one day when we stand in His presence, holy and pure in all the beauty He planned. Speaking of God's people, the Lord says that "a book of remembrance was written before him for them that feared the LORD, and that thought upon his name. And they shall be mine, saith the LORD of hosts, in that day when I make up my jewels" (Malachi 3:16–17 KJV). You will not always be a "diamond in the rough." God has plans for you—for all eternity!

| **Cry from my Heart** | *Lord, thank You for seeing me as a flawless gem! Thank You that I can trust You with everything that happens in my life, knowing that Your work is painstakingly perfect!* |

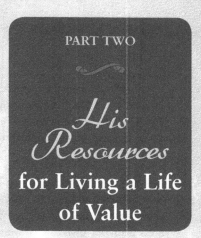

PART TWO

His
Resources
for Living a Life
of Value

VALUE (noun): the regard that
something is held to deserve;
the importance, worth, or
usefulness of something

Synonyms: advantage, benefit,
gain, profit, good, help, merit,
helpfulness, significance, cost

$\mathscr{A}$ Word about Resources

You are a person of great value. That's exactly
how God sees you. What's more, when He
fashioned you, He had a purpose in mind—that
you would be all He created you to be. But He
doesn't expect you to do it all on your own.

Jesus said, "I am the vine; you are the branches. . . .
Apart from me you can do nothing" (John 15:5).
So it's important for us to realize we can't make
it on our own. Because we just don't have what
it takes on our own to deal with the crises of
life, we shouldn't expect that from ourselves.
God knew we would need resources far beyond
what we have if we were ever going to be all He
created us to be.

God has not left you on this earth without what
you need to make the most of who you are.
He provides you with forgiveness, peace,
strength, contentment, intimacy with Himself,
and so much more.

In Part Two we'll take a look at some of these
amazing, inexhaustible resources God makes
available for His daughters. I have a feeling these
reserves may be just what you're needing!

His Pardon—
Total Forgiveness

"I wish I could believe what you said tonight is really true," a lady commented to the pastor at the end of the service. He had spoken of God's forgiveness, but the sadness in her eyes showed she had not accepted the truth he had spoken about. With tears filling her eyes, she went on, "What I have done is so bad, I can never forgive myself."

Every one of us has done things we regret. We have all had to live with the consequences of our appalling actions at one time or another. But when a woman says she cannot forgive herself, she needs to understand several concepts:

1   To forgive yourself does not mean to say, "It's okay, what I did wasn't so bad after all." All the rationalizing in the world doesn't change the

fact that sin is wrong. Recognizing this is an important step if you are ever to forgive yourself.

2   Be sure you have dealt with your sin in a Biblical way. Make sure your <u>confession to</u> God has been full and sincere. Are you sorry you sinned, or are you merely sorry you got caught? Half measures will never do. You see, all sin is ultimately sin against God. When David sinned with <u>Bathshe</u>ba, he admitted to God, "<u>Agains</u>t <u>you, you only, have I sinned</u>" (<u>Psalm 5</u>1:4). Any sin <u>against one of God's children is</u> sin against God; we must have His forgiveness to restore fellowship. But you cannot confess to God alone when you should also confess to someone else. Here's something that might help you.

> **Secret** sins should be secretly confessed to God. If the sin is an area of <u>continu</u>ing temptation, it should be confessed to a person who is safe and will covenant to <u>pray with you</u> and <u>hold you</u> account<u>able for resisting the sin.</u>

> **Private** sins should be privately confessed between you and the person involved.

> **Public** sins should be publicly confessed.

3   You must know whether or not God has really forgiven you before you can truly forgive yourself. Usually the woman who says she cannot forgive herself does not have a true understanding of God's forgiveness. We need to remember the basis of God's forgiveness is not merely because He loves us (an emotional response), but because of a concrete event in history—the death of Jesus on the cross. John 3:16 does not say, "God so loved the world that whoever believes in him may have everlasting life." It's the giving of His Son as our substitute that makes God just in forgiving us. Whenever you doubt if God has forgiven you, look back to Calvary and remember that it is a physical event in history—a fact.

To forgive yourself, you must understand that not only does God cleanse us, but He also restores us to a place of being "chaste" or "pure virgins" in His sight. In his book *The Mary Miracle,* Dr. Jack Hayford points out that in the ancient Roman world, the word "Corinthian" was a common adjective for being "rotten to the core." Corinth, located in present-day Greece, was known for its sin.

In Paul's first letter to the Christians of
Corinth, he lists some pretty wayward charac-
ters: the sexually immoral, idolaters, adulterers,
male prostitutes, homosexual offenders, thieves,
the greedy, drunkards, slanderers, and swin-
dlers. Then he personalizes it by saying, "And
that is what some of you were."

Then comes the good news: "But you were
washed, you were sanctified, you were justified
in the name of the Lord Jesus Christ and by the
Spirit of our God" (1 Corinthians 6:11). It is
already wonderful to be washed, sanctified, and
clean. But in his second letter to the Corinthians,
Paul adds an even more astounding thought:
"I am jealous for you with a godly jealousy. I
promised you to one husband, to Christ, so that
I might present you as a *pure virgin* to him" (2
Corinthians 11:2, italics mine).

Hayford says,

> Do you hear that, dear one? *A chaste
> virgin.* Look at this awesome new
> creation statement in God's Word! See
> how former sin and sex addicts are
> now being declared "virginal"! Can
> you imagine a more towering statement
> on how vast the possibilities of God's

restorative powers are, once He sets
about recovering ruined, broken, or
sin-stained people?[33]

What a magnificent thought!

Yet, in spite of all that Scripture says, how often the memory of our sins is brought before us and we confess them again and ask forgiveness again! Yet when we confess sins that God has already forgiven, to whom are we confessing? To God? Is He the one reminding us of past sins? Does He bring up again what He has so freely and fully forgiven? Does He remember what He has forgotten? Jeremiah 31:34 says: "For I will forgive their wickedness and will remember their sins no more." Did you get that: *no more!*

According to the Bible, who, then, is the one who accuses us of being sinners? Who would keep us under constant condemnation? Satan! He's called "the accuser of our brothers . . . who accuses them before our God day and night" (Revelation 12:10). If I continue to confess a sin that God has forgiven and forgotten, I am only confessing it to the "accuser of our brothers," the Devil.

Instead of taking our stand against his accusations, we believe him instead of God. We refuse to forgive ourselves because we believe the Enemy's accusations of guilt. We continue to punish ourselves, thinking, "This is what I deserve!"

When we do this, we minimize the grace of God, who tells us, "For it is by grace you have been saved, through faith—and this is not from yourselves, it is the gift of God—not by works, so that no one can boast" (Ephesians 2:8–9). We doubt the cleansing power of the blood of Jesus, through whom "we have redemption through his blood, the forgiveness of sins, in accordance with the riches of God's grace that he lavished on us" (Ephesians 1:7–8).

We also humiliate ourselves before Satan, elevating him to a place of influence over us that God never intended. We destroy our faith and confidence in the Lord. John tells us we must be free from condemnation if we are to have confidence toward God: "Dear friends, if our hearts do not condemn us, we have confidence before God and receive from him anything we ask, because we keep his commands and do what pleases him" (1 John 3:21–22). We *can* have that confidence:

> Therefore, brothers and sisters, since
> we have confidence to enter the Most
> Holy Place by the blood of Jesus, by
> a new and living way opened for us
> through the curtain, that is, his body,
> and since we have a great priest over
> the house of God, let us draw near to
> God and with the full assurance that
> faith brings, having our hearts sprinkled
> to cleanse us from a guilty conscience
> and having our bodies washed with
> pure water. Let us hold unswervingly to
> the hope we profess, for he who prom-
> ised is faithful. *(Hebrews 10:19–23)*

And finally, we forget that we are children of
God: "See what kind of love the Father has
lavished on us, that we should be called children
of God! And that is what we are!" (1 John 3:1).
Would a loving parent want to continually
remind his daughter that she had "messed up"?
Only a bad parent does that.

If you have confessed sin to God and to any
other appropriate person, then don't confess it
again, for you would probably be confessing to
the Devil. Thousands of Christians are torment-
ing themselves because they will not forgive
themselves.

What does it mean to forgive yourself? It means you give up your right to punish yourself for what you have done wrong. If God forgives me (and He does!), who am I to refuse to forgive myself?

Let me tell you about Cathy. My husband was called to the hospital to pray for her baby, who was not expected to live beyond age two because she had five holes in her tiny heart. As Cathy's precious little girl lay in a crib, she turned to Harold and with scalding tears asked, "Why is God punishing my baby for what I did? God is punishing me for the life I lived before I was a Christian."

When Cathy was growing up, her mom would always picture God to her as a bully with a big club who was out to get her every time she did wrong. When she reached the teen years, in rebellion against her mom, Cathy decided she was going to have her fun no matter what, and she had a series of sexual relationships. Eventually she married. But things went wrong. A Kansas spring flood filled her family's basement and they lost almost everything they had. Then a child was stillborn. And now this baby was not expected to live past two. Whenever anything bad happened to her, Cathy was certain God was punishing her for the life she had lived before she was a Christian.

Cathy had become a believer several years before. One day, as she was walking down the street, she heard music coming from a building, saw it was a church, and went inside. There she heard the gospel message that God loved her and offered forgiveness for her sins. She accepted Jesus as her personal Savior that day. But she had never been able to feel confident that her past was wiped clean.

Was God punishing her through all the heartbreaks she had experienced? Not if you believe what the Bible says about forgiveness: "I, yes, I alone am he who blots away your sins for my own sake and will never think of them again" (Isaiah 43:25 TLB).

Harold prayed God would heal this tiny baby so Cathy would know that when God forgives, He forgets. And God answered that prayer. The last time we had contact with the family, Cathy's daughter was a young adult enjoying excellent health.

Are you struggling with forgiving yourself for something you have done? Write that sin on a piece of paper. Then picture that piece of paper nailed to the cross of Jesus and being covered with His blood that paid the penalty for our sins. The Bible tells us that's exactly what happened to our sins: "When you were dead in your sins . . . God made you alive with Christ . . . having canceled the charge of our legal indebtedness, which stood against us and condemned us; he has taken it away, nailing it to the cross" (Colossians 2:13–14). You may even want to burn that piece of paper.

When you know God has forgiven you of all your sins, you will gain a sense of how precious you are to Him.

Cry **from my Heart**

Thank You that my sins are gone—washed away by Your precious blood.

His Presence, His Power, His Pleasure—
God's Resources for You

To me the most thrilling truth in the Bible is that the great God of the universe loves me. Incredible! How could He ever love us enough to endure such awful suffering in our place? If on the bumpy road of life you ever start to doubt God's love for you, just think back to what is probably the most familiar verse in the Bible: John 3:16, for that gives us assurance: "For God so loved the world that he gave his one and only Son, that whoever believes in him shall not perish but have eternal life."

But now let's take that thought one step further. If God gave Jesus for us, will He not also supply everything else we need? I mean, Jesus was the *ultimate* gift any of us could receive. So won't God give us everything else we need as well? Actually, that's almost exactly what Paul tells us: "He who did not spare his own Son, but gave him up for us all—how will he not also, along with him, graciously give us all things?" (Romans 8:32). If God did not keep back His *most* precious gift, the gift of His Son, what makes you think He will hesitate to give you anything else you might need to fulfill His purpose for you?

But you live in a very real world. You have problems to solve and difficulties to cope with that are unique to you. In all probability you didn't get yesterday's To Do List checked off— let alone today's. Perhaps you have a large payment due on your home and you wonder where the money is going to come from. Or you have serious issues in your marriage. Your son or daughter is in trouble. Or it could be a doctor's appointment you're worried about. What resources does God have to meet the problems you face today? How can you be sure God will be there for you?

Let's take a look at Zephaniah 3:16–17 (NIV 1984): "Do not fear, O Zion; do not let your hands hang limp. The LORD your God is with you, he is mighty to save. He will take great delight in you; he will quiet you with his love, he will rejoice over you with singing."

Got limp hands today? A tired body? Need extra strength to cope? Notice that in these short verses are three provisions or resources just for you:

- God's **presence** with you

- His **power** for you

- His **pleasure** in you

His Presence with You

Did you notice that Zephaniah said, "The Lord your God is with you"?

At one time or another you probably have seen the poem called "Footprints in the Sand."[34] Mary Stevenson wrote it in 1936 when she was sixteen years old.

In the poem, she tells about a dream that she had where she was walking on the beach with the Lord. In the dream, many scenes from her life flashed across the sky. In each scene she noticed footprints in the sand. Sometimes there were two sets of footprints. This bothered her because she noticed that during the low periods of her life, there was only one set of footprints.

So Mary said to the Lord, "You promised me, Lord, if I followed You, You would walk with me always. But I noticed that during the most trying periods of my life, there has been only one set of prints in the sand. Why, when I needed You most, have You not been there for me?"

The Lord replied, "The times when you have seen only one set of footprints is when I carried you."

Now, I used to feel that was a nice thought, but when people put words in God's mouth, how do I know they're true? That is—until I came across Deuteronomy 1:31, where Moses told the Israelites: "You saw how the LORD your God carried you, as a father carries his son, all the way you went until you reached this place."

When Moses said those words, the Israelites stood poised on the very edge of the Promised Land that would eventually become Israel. They had covered many miles from Egypt across the Red Sea and the Sinai Desert. God had obviously brought them to this point. But God says that across those many desolate miles, He had actually been carrying them.

Now, did it always *feel* like God was carry-

ing them? What about when they were cornered
at the Red Sea? In front of them lay the sea. On
each side were mountains. Behind them they
could hear the thundering hooves of the horses
and the chariots of Egypt in hot pursuit. God
gave them a miraculous deliverance through the
Red Sea on dry land, but for a while it certainly
didn't *feel* like they were riding on God's
shoulders.

Only three days after this great event, the
Israelites were intensely thirsty. Finally they
came to water, but it turned out to be bitter.
Again they doubted God. But God came through
for them and made the water drinkable.

And that wasn't the last time they felt
discouraged. Six weeks after they had left Egypt,
they were getting tired of picnics. " 'If only we
had died by the LORD's hand in Egypt!" they
complained. "There we sat around pots of meat
and ate all the food we wanted, but you [Moses]
have brought us out into this desert to starve
this entire assembly to death'" (Exodus 16:3).
Did that feel like God was carrying them?
Not at all. Yet God miraculously supplied manna
for them to eat.

And how did they respond? Well, just let
me interject here that God knows what it's like

when your children complain about their food.
After God provided manna, before the Israelites could climb the next sand dune, they were
complaining that manna wasn't enough. They
wanted meat. But even when God supplied
quail, they still complained.

Can't you just hear them—"This sun's hot.
The sand burns my feet. I'm sick and tired of living
out of a backpack. All we have to eat is manna
and quail, manna and quail, manna and quail."

And so it went, month after month. The
people complained. But God went right on
providing and protecting, as a good father does.
Never *once* did He leave them. He was there
as a pillar of cloud by day and a pillar of fire
by night, carrying them on His shoulders. His
presence was with them, just as Zephaniah said.

What Moses told the Israelites is what God
is saying to you today: "Be strong and coura-
geous. Do not be afraid or terrified because of
them, for the LORD your God goes with you;
he will never leave you nor forsake you. . . . Do
not be afraid; do not be discouraged" (Deuteronomy 31:6, 8).

Dear friend, the Lord your God is with you.
You may not always feel like He's there, but
don't trust your feelings. Jesus said, "Surely I

am with you always, to the very end of the age"
(Matthew 28:20). "Never will I leave you; never
will I forsake you" (Hebrews 13:5).

He is in you, if you are His child. The Apostle Paul wrote, "Don't you know that you yourselves are God's temple and that God's Spirit
dwells in your midst?" (1 Corinthians 3:16).
John assured us that "the one who is in you is
greater than the one who is in the world" (1 John
4:4).

In the work of Guidelines International
Ministries, my husband and I travel overseas a
good deal—and a lot of the places we visit are
not safe. People ask us if we're afraid to travel.
Harold's response is always: "Safety is not the
absence of danger but the presence of the Lord."

One of my favorite verses is Isaiah 41:10:
"'Do not fear, for I am with you; do not be
dismayed, for I am your God. I will strengthen
you and help you; I will uphold you with my
righteous right hand." When I was a very little
girl and my Dad took me on walks, I would
grasp one of his big fingers so I wouldn't fall.
But my Dad knew that was not enough because
my hands were so tiny. So, although I was holding on to him, he would wrap his big fingers

around my hand so that if I let go, He would still be holding on to me.

Never forget that although you may let go of God, He will still be holding on to you. The Lord your God is with you. You can count on it.

His Power for You

Not only is God's presence with you, His power is for you. Zephaniah says, "He is mighty to save." I like to think about the power of God. Jeremiah says, "Sovereign LORD, you have made the heavens and the earth by your great power and outstretched arm. Nothing is too hard for you" (32:17). We serve a mighty God!

Whenever I lose perspective, I like to look at the night sky—the sparkling stars, the brilliant moon, the planets, and the constellations. The One who made those—as the song goes, "He knows my name, He knows my every thought!" Yes, the world I see around me is a reminder of His greatness, this God I love and serve.

Here's an interesting verse in Isaiah: "For this is what the LORD says—he who created the heavens, he is God; he who fashioned and made the earth, he founded it; he did not create it to be empty, but formed it to be inhabited" (Isaiah

45:18). That verse contains no small truth. Why is it significant? For one thing, even with our powerful telescopes, man has never found another planet in the universe that is suitable to support human life. Ours is covered with vegetation, oceans, rivers, mountains, deserts, land masses, and half a million islands. The surface of most planets is barren and dull, but ours was formed to be inhabited. Some type of life is found on every spot on earth. Even in extremely cold Antarctica, you can find microscopic beings, tiny insects, and even two types of plants that flower every year. From the top of the atmosphere surrounding our planet to the bottom of the oceans, life persists.[35] Our God is powerful!

If the earth moved closer to the sun or farther away, we would either burn up or freeze. Yet, did you know that if the moon were much nearer to the earth than it is, we would experience huge tides that would overflow onto the lowlands? Eventually the oceans would cover the earth a mile and a half deep. Our mighty God is the one who planned it all. He keeps the sun, the moon, and the oceans in balance to support life.

And we haven't even considered cool, clear water. The earth is the only planet we know whose surface is 70-percent covered with water. In the daytime, the oceans absorb large amounts of heat, keeping the rest of the earth fairly cool. At night, the oceans release the heat soaked up during the day, and this heat keeps the earth from getting too cold. If it were not for the huge amount of water on the earth, many parts would be so hot that water would boil in the daytime and then freeze at night. Our vast oceans are a vital part of our survival. Yet, as far as we know, ours is the only planet covered with that much water.

The chances of our planet being just right for life are extremely minute. The odds that this happened by chance are astronomical—something like billions to one!

Yet, that said, the earth we live on is a very little thing to God. Isaiah asks:

> Who has measured the waters in the
>   hollow of his hand,
> or with the breadth of his hand marked
>   off the heavens?
> Who has held the dust of the earth in
>   a basket,
> or weighed the mountains on the scales

> and the hills in a balance? *(Isaiah 40:12)*

Nevertheless, we often let worry get the best of us. Corrie ten Boom, that indomitable Dutch lady who survived the cruel inhumanity of the Ravensbrück concentration camp in WW2, once said: "When I worry I go to the mirror and say to myself, 'This tremendous thing which is worrying me is beyond a solution. It is especially too hard for Jesus Christ to handle.' After I have said that, I smile and I am ashamed."[36]

We serve a mighty God. As Zephaniah says, He is powerful to save! Nothing we face is bigger than our heavenly Father!

His Pleasure in You

Zephaniah 3:17 assures us, "He will take great delight in you." Psalm 149:4 says, "For the LORD takes delight in his people."

God created us. But He didn't stop there. He delights in us. When your baby was born, did you take one look at him or her and say, "Wow, that's wonderful!" and then turn and walk away, leaving him in the hospital? No! You eagerly took that little baby home and began to nurture him or her. You took delight in your baby day after day. Is God any less of a parent?

Where did the idea of parenting begin, anyway? With God! He is the Supreme Parent who cares for His children. He delights in us. We're not a burden to Him.

I had the joy of being in the delivery room when our son's first baby was born. With Cheryl's biological clock ticking and a history of miscarriages, this baby was very precious. They didn't want to know ahead of time if the baby was a boy or girl, but I knew Steve was hoping for a son. When Steve first saw Christian, he said with great joy, "It's a boy!" He wouldn't leave the hospital. He slept that night in a chair in Cheryl's room.

The next morning, when Cheryl came out of the shower, she saw Steve holding baby Christian on his lap—with tears streaming down his face. He was taking delight in his son. That's a picture of the delight God takes in us, His kids.

Now look at the next phrase in Zephaniah: "He will quiet you with his love." Have you ever had a time when your baby wouldn't stop crying? I have—and it's frightening. How did I stop my baby from crying? Did I plop her in the crib and walk out of the room? No! I picked her up, wrapped her tightly, and held her close as

I walked the floor with her. I cuddled her and rubbed her back, and assured her of my love.

I would go so far as to say that every day, we, too, need to climb up on God's lap, so to speak, and let Him quiet us with His love. You may be facing a situation right now where everything is chaos. You don't know which way to turn. Before you make any decision, take time to be still. Focus on the fact that God loves you even more than a mother loves her own child. Let Him calm your heart and assure you that He cares for you.

The last phrase of those Zephaniah verses says: "He will rejoice over you with singing." Until I read that, I didn't know God sings! We sing praises to God. But here is the great God Almighty singing over us because He loves us so much and delights in us, just as I sang over my little ones out of sheer joy.

When I think of this, it transforms prayer for me. Instead of prayer being the presentation of a Things I Want list to God, it becomes an intimate time of companionship and joy, sharing my heart with Him and He with me. Some of the best prayer times are when we don't use words—we just sit in His presence.

Eric Liddell was a Scottish runner who won a gold medal in the Olympics of 1924. His story was memorialized in the Oscar-winning movie *Chariots of Fire*. Born in China to missionary parents but educated in England and Scotland, Eric was an outstanding athlete. He was a staunch Christian who refused to run races on Sundays. When he learned that his best event, the 100-meter race, was to be on a Sunday, he switched to the 400-meter race, and though this was not his strongest event, with God's help he won. Later he returned to China as a missionary, dying of illness in a WW2 Japanese internment camp.

Before the Olympic Games, Eric's sister had urged him to give up running and get on with his life's work as a missionary. Eric's response to her was that at this point in his life, he felt God wanted him to run.

"God made me fast, and when I run I feel His pleasure," Eric told her.

How do you give God pleasure? Exactly the same way—as you fulfill His will for your life. What is it God wants you to do—that thing that you've been resisting? Make the decision today to say YES to His plan, and you, too, will give God pleasure. He will rejoice over you with singing!

Remember, whatever problems you face, God has promised to give you the resources you need to accomplish His purpose for you. You are more precious than diamonds to Him. He will give us:

* His presence with us,

* His power for us,

and

* His pleasure in us.

Say yes to Him today. Then go out with the assurance that He will use you to accomplish what He has put you on this earth to do.

Cry **from my Heart**

I'm so needy today, Lord. I want to draw from Your resources for all my deficiencies.

His Peace
—Coping with the Problem Women Don't Talk About:
DEPRESSION

(A study of Psalm 42 and 43)

Someone once said there are two good things about being depressed:

1 You never have to make your bed, because you're always in it.

2 You always have your funeral planned in advance.

Not too long ago, when I was with a group of women who were leaders in their churches, I brought up the subject of depression. The room grew silent. Almost in a whisper one of them said to me, "We don't talk about that."

"I know we don't. But we should," I replied.
"We're leaving women to struggle alone on
dark days when we who know God's resources
should come alongside and walk with them."
Unfortunately, in some Christian circles depression is looked upon as a deficiency in spiritual-
ity. "If you just really trusted God, you'd be able
to snap out of your depression," these women
are told. Seeing a psychiatrist, even a Christian
one, is considered a lack of faith.

In the closing months of my own mother's
life, she struggled with dementia for which
her Christian doctor prescribed medication.
"Shouldn't I be able to find God's help to overcome this without taking medication?" she asked
me. I told her that when we have something
wrong with us physically such as an infection,
we don't hesitate to take antibiotics. Why is it
wrong, then, to take medication that helps us
cope with a mental condition—when for whatever reason our brains aren't working right?

Let's be honest. We've all gotten depressed
at one time or another. Personally, I'm prone to
depression when I get home from an overseas
ministry trip and jet lag sets in. Once, about
five days after returning home from ministry

in Cuba, I said to my daughter Bonnie: "I'm a mess. I'm not worth *any*thing!"

"You mean you're not getting anything done, Mom."

Yes, Bonnie, you're right. I realized I tend to equate worth with accomplishment and get depressed when I can't finish items on my To Do list.

But that's a minor problem compared with the deep depression some women experience. They feel trapped by their circumstances. Even trapped by their own psychoses.

Depression impacts every area of our lives—social life, family, work, ministry, and our self-worth. For women, depression is actually common. In fact, women are about two times more likely to suffer depression than men are.

Depression can sometimes be a form of repressed anger—anger turned inward. At times we find ourselves in situations where we can't show anger or think we shouldn't. We wouldn't dare. We're Christians! We think, "I'm supposed to love people, not get mad at them! Besides that, I read my Bible—shouldn't that be enough?" So we stuff our anger and get more deeply depressed than ever.

Yet sometimes depression is the opposite of anger. It is a state of inertia and utter hopelessness. During those times, we'd be happy to stay in bed and pull the blanket up over our head. We're not sure we even want to live.

Depression can also be brought on because of loss, such as that of a dear friend or family member—or even a pet. Loss of possessions or income can cause depression as well. We have the feeling that we can't control most aspects of our lives.

Another loss we don't often think of as causing depression is the loss of self-esteem. Perhaps we've had a change of responsibilities at work or in ministry, and we don't feel we fit our new position.

Depression can also be brought on by physical problems. Chemical imbalance can cause clinical depression. So can fatigue, lack of exercise, poor health, poor diet, illness, and a physical condition such as low blood sugar. Even certain medications have side effects of depression.

All of this was brought home to me in a personal way when our Philippines ministry partner Maricar Flores-Alvarez suffered from depression. I'm delighted that Maricar was willing to open up about the problem she faced and, in doing so, can be an encouragement to others.

❀ ❀ ❀

It's Not Just in My Head
by Maricar Flores-Alvarez

For most of my life, I have always been healthy—and by "healthy" I mean heavy! As a student, little regard to proper nutrition and exercise made me a regular at our school clinic and later, as an employee, led me to constantly being on sick leave.

As a teen, I was diagnosed with Polycystic Ovarian Syndrome (PCOS), a metabolic condition that commonly causes hormonal imbalances in women. This figured significantly in my inability to get pregnant when I got married, causing my hormones to play tricks with my emotions, with feelings of inadequacy and failure. This was my first glimpse of depression.

In 2005, I suffered a slipped disc in my lower back, pinching the largest nerve on my spine and causing excruciating pain to shoot down my right leg. After over a year of therapy and medication, I eventually strengthened my back and learned to manage the pain. However, this only added to the bleakness of our dream to have a baby.

Finally, after seven years, the Lord answered our prayers and granted us a son, Adrian. As happy as we could possibly be as first-time parents, I felt differently a few days later. My hormones were playing tricks on my emotions again, giving me feelings of insecurity, guilt, and dread. In spite of all this, I simply refused to acknowledge that I needed help.

Two years later, the Lord blessed us with another baby boy: Azriel. Early on in my pregnancy, my husband, Amor, had warned me that it was possible that I could have the exact same feelings I had had when Adrian was born. This time, we called it what it really was: postpartum depression.

Unfortunately, I developed full-on depression several months later when I had debilitating feelings of hopelessness—as if it were completely impossible for me to ever recover. At one point, I felt that Amor and the kids would be better off without me, and I contemplated ending it all so I would not be a burden to them anymore.

With depression complicating my hormones, my emotions were going haywire—it was difficult for people to be around me! There were many days I was cranky, irritable, and easily set off by the slightest insignificant things. Unfortunately, Amor was often on the receiving end of my outbursts.

After having two kids, I longed to start each day vibrant and energetic. I wanted to engage in sports with Amor. I wanted to run and play with the boys. People had no idea how many times I cried in bed because I had pain in my back, some sort of discomfort in my stomach, or because I was simply depleted and defeated.

I thank the Lord for Amor and his quiet resolve. He stood by me through it all and urged me to seek help. We both spent lots of time with Dr. Sala and Darlene, opening up about what we were going through. Amor also accompanied me to a psychiatrist, who was also a believer in Christ, and she explained my condition. For the next few months, Amor joined me in therapy and assured me that he was with me every step of the way. He also encouraged me to open up about my feelings and talk to people. More importantly, he always encouraged me to keep praying and keep reading God's Word—whether I felt like it or not!

In 2011 I met more health challenges, with a diagnosis of gallstones, fatty liver, hypertension,

and pre-diabetes. We feared I would have to
have surgery. But instead of taking conventional
medicine and treatments, I made the decision to
change my lifestyle by making healthier dietary
choices and adopting a low-impact workout.

Within a year, I lost a total of forty-five
pounds and now I feel great! I am more active
and my health has dramatically improved! And
since Amor and the kids have made a similar
change in their lifestyle, they too have barely
been sick and have gone without medication
for over a year! Through this experience, many
doors have opened up for me to minister to
others, sharing with them that being good stew-
ards of our bodies is a personal act of worship
to the Lord!

❀ ❀ ❀

When facing emotional problems, what book
in the Bible are we most likely to turn to? I'm
sure you'd agree with me that it's the book of
Psalms. Why? Probably because the Psalms deal
with every condition, every emotion, of the
human heart.

When I'm depressed, two of my favorite
chapters to read are Psalms 42 and 43—the ones
where the psalmist asks himself, "Why are you

downcast, O my soul?" We're going to look at six steps the psalmist used to get out of a "funk."

These two psalms may have been one psalm originally. Notice that the final verse of each is identical. We don't know who wrote them, but they were probably written as a song. In these chapters the psalmist talks to God, then talks to himself, then talks to God—back and forth, just like many of our prayers.

The psalmist's condition

If you read these two psalms in several translations of the Bible and make a list of the negative words and phrases the writer uses, you will find a pretty thorough description of his condition: *thirst, downcast, agony, taunting, tears, despair, mourning, disturbed, weeping, crying, disquieted, cast down, sunk down, discouraged, oppressed, reproached, rejected.* If you weren't depressed already, that list is enough to make you depressed!

It's important to tell God exactly how you feel. Don't rush through this process. Psalm 142:2 says, "I pour out before him my complaint; before him I tell my trouble." Lamentations 2:19 says, "Pour out your heart like water in the

presence of the Lord." In other words, acknowledge that you have a problem, and tell God all
the details.

We tend to pray nice prayers to God and
then take out our true feelings on those we
live with. We pray, "Thank You so much, God,
for Your wonderful goodness to me." And five
minutes later we're yelling at our kids, "Why
can't you listen to me! I'm so sick of your attitude!" If you've got anger inside, express it to
God. He's big enough to take it. Pour out what's
in your heart to Him instead of taking it out on
those around you.

One thing I notice in these psalms is that
the writer longs for God; he thirsts for Him. He
pants for Him as an animal craves water. But
God seems far away. One evening my husband
and I attended a Bible study where the pastor
was teaching on these two psalms. He was reading the second verse of Psalm 42, "My soul
thirsts for God, for the living God. When can I
go and meet with God?" Loudly, a little boy in
the audience called out, "Right now!" The boy
was right, though sometimes our circumstances
are so bad that we're hesitant to come to Him.

Then notice that the psalmist feels forsaken by God. In Psalm 42:9 he asks, "Why have you forgotten me?" In Psalm 43:2 he adds, "Why have you rejected me?" Can you identify with his feelings? The children of Israel felt that way, too, at one point: "The LORD has forsaken me, the LORD has forgotten me" (Isaiah 49:14). The writer of Psalm 10 declares in despair, "God will never notice; he covers his face and never sees" (verse 11).

The third condition in these psalms is that the writer feels overwhelmed by his circumstances: "All your waves and breakers have swept over me" (Psalm 42:7). At this point the psalmist remembers the good times of the past: "These things I remember as I pour out my soul: how I used to go to the house of God under the protection of the Mighty One with shouts of joy and praise among the festive throng" (Psalm 42:4). The human tendency is to remember the good and forget the bad. We remember the good times we had at home growing up—and forget the family feuds. We remember wonderful Christmases together—and forget the bitter argument and hurt feelings we had last year over whose house we were going to for dinner.

Then the psalmist asks the question, "When shall I come and appear before God?" What mother has not thought of Psalm 55:6? "Oh, that I had the wings of a dove! I would fly away and be at rest." When we're depressed, any place sounds better than where we are now. But some think the psalmist's desire to appear before God may have been a desire to die—a suicide wish, for suicide is a very real danger in times of severe depression. No statement a person makes regarding the desire to die should ever be taken lightly; it should be recognized as a call for help. If you have any thoughts along these lines, let me urge you to get professional help as soon as possible. You are too precious to risk tragedy.

Don't think there is no hope for you. That's the way my friend Carol felt.

> I stared vacantly at the black tote bag that was hidden inside my closet. No one would even be curious about it if they saw it, for it was just an old tote bag with a broken zipper, ragged, nondescript . . . just like me. *There is an answer to all of this sadness,* I would think, *and everything I need to escape is inside this bag.*

Alone in my room with the bag, I would begin the "Ritual of the Bottles." I had been exceptionally pleased lately, for I had a new addition to my collection of thirty-plus bottles of pills. Incredibly, I had never taken any of the pills (and there were hundreds of them), but I would periodically take the bottles out and look at them, lining them up on my bed as some people might their jewelry. Looking at them in their properly labeled safety-capped containers, I would think about how, where, why—and when.

The when . . . that was the problem. I became distressed when I thought of my children finding me dead, for although I was convinced they no longer needed me in their lives, as their mother I still had enough emotional strength to think about wanting to spare them that agony.

I had a plan and a secret weapon known only to me. I never considered for one bleak moment that God also had a plan for me.

My life had become unbearable after both my parents and my two best friends died of cancer and my marriage ended. The weight of all the losses and accompanying stresses crushed me. Fearing God's judgment

didn't seem to be an issue. I truly believed
He knew me best and that He understood
that I was broken beyond repair. He would
understand, I thought, and if not—well, I
would take my chances with Him. After all,
He was the God who loved me enough to
die for me. Surely He would be compassion-
ate with me.

But, beside the pills, I kept something
else in the bag—my journals. I had a sizable
collection of journals in which I had been
penning my thoughts, my dialogues with
God, and records of innumerable answered
prayers. The pills were my answer, but the
journals were God's answer!

One dark December day, I picked up
and read my entire journal of the year my
friend Steph died. I read page after page,
relentlessly sobbing and doing the grieving I
had never done. God reminded me of Psalm
56:8: "You have kept count of my tossings;
put my tears in your bottle. Are they not
in your book?" (Psalm 56:8 ESV). When it
was over, God had won the battle. I calmly
got up from my bed, went to the closet, and
flushed away the pills, along with long years
of pent-up sorrow.

The journals? Well, they eventually became a book. I went on to discover deep fulfillment, not only in writing for the Lord, but also in living the life He has always intended me to live. Have I continued to experience sorrows? I've seen five more of my loved ones succumb to cancer, one to murder, and others suffer life-threatening illnesses. But God promises to be with me whether I go up to the mountaintop or down into the deepest desert valley. Had I taken my life, His plan for me would have been thwarted. God is the Restorer of my life, my mind, and my spirit.

The psalmist's six-step treatment for recovery

Let's look at six steps the psalmist used to treat his depression:

1   **He verbalizes his feelings to God in all honesty.** "My tears have been my food day and night, while people say to me all day long, 'Where is your God?'" (Psalm 42:3).

2   He remembers what God has done for him
    in the past.

"My soul is downcast within me; therefore I will
remember you" (Psalm 42:6). What has God
done for you? Do you remember when He saved
you, healed you, or that time He answered your
prayer about a big need? Keeping some sort of
journal of the high points in your life can be a
tremendous encouragement when you are going
through a down period.

3   He makes a decision to praise God.

He says, "For I will yet praise him"(Psalm 43:5).
That takes faith when you're depressed. But
here are tools to help you.

* Make a playlist of praise music you
  enjoy. Sing or just listen. Music that
  glorifies God will touch your heart
  when sermons leave you cold.

* Scripture on your tablet or phone is also
  good. "I lie in the dust; revive me by
  your word" (Psalm 119:25 NLT), says
  the psalmist to God. If you've always
  read Scripture but never listened to it,
  try it. You'll notice truths that you may
  have skipped over when reading. By the
  way, most of the downloads are free.

* Someone once said: "Praise is the only shortcut to victory." I believe it's also one of the most effective shortcuts out of depression.

4   He focuses on who God is.

Because of who God is, we praise, not because we are pleased with the circumstances of our lives. In these chapters there are seven names for God.

* 42:2 Living God—He is not dead like the gods of other religions.

* 42:8 God of my life—He keeps me going.

* 42:9 God my rock—He is solid, indestructible.

* 42:11 Help of my countenance. Most of our "countenances" could use some help!

* 43:2 God of my strength—my stronghold. He is my strength when mine runs out.

* 43:4 My exceeding joy.

* 43:4 MY God—not just the God of the
  Bible.

Try this tomorrow morning. The instant you
wake up, ask yourself this question: "What do I
know to be true about God today?" Write down
your answer on your calendar or a Post-it or a
scrap of paper, and take that thought with you
throughout your day. You may be surprised what
an encouragement it will be.

5 He prays for God's light and truth to lead him
   (Psalm 43:3).
What does God's light do for us? It illuminates
the next step in the darkness of our depression.
How we need Him to clearly direct us when
we feel hopeless! And what does His truth do?
It reshapes our warped perspective so we see
issues in their proper proportion. The problem
that looks impossible is cut down to size when
we apply the truth of God's Word to it, the
God who says, "What is impossible with man
is possible with God" (Luke 18:27). "Guide my
steps by your word," you may cry out, "so I will
not be overcome by evil" (Psalm 119:133 NLT).

And where will God's light and truth lead you? To a fresh encounter with Him. Note the progress the psalmist makes in Psalm 43:3–4:

- "Send me your light and your faithful care, let them lead me . . . to your holy mountain, to the place where you dwell." You can see that he's headed in God's direction now.

- "Then I will go to the altar of God"— the altar is the place where he would meet God.

- "To God my joy and delight. I will praise you with the lyre, O God, my God." Already his attitude seems to have changed.

6 He verbalizes his faith.

"Put your hope in God, for I will yet praise him, my Savior and my God." Three times in these two chapters you find these exact words (42:5, 11; 43:5). What an assertion of faith! The psalmist believed God was going to take him through the dark valley and bring him to a place of victory over the depression he was experiencing—and he said so by faith.

When my friend Debbie was diagnosed with multiple sclerosis, her husband left her and their two daughters. Debbie told the girls she was angry with God because not only did she have this terrible disease, but now she had a broken home as well. "Is it okay to say to the girls that I'm mad at God?" she asked me. I told her that of course it was okay to verbalize her feelings to God and the girls, but that she must also verbalize her faith. That she should say, "With God's help, we *will* get through this—God will bring us through." As the writer of Psalms 42 and 43 would say, "We will yet praise Him."

Let me add one more thought. Depression can also be caused by stuffing things in the closet of your heart and refusing to deal with them. Anger, hurt, bitterness, and unforgiveness are deadly if not acknowledged. Worry about the future can cause depression as well. The pain of abuse in the past can produce long-term depression unless it is dealt with. Perhaps it is time to clean out the closet of your life. There *is* forgiveness, healing, and resolution with God.

Then you can say with the psalmist (Psalm 43:5): "Why, my soul, are you downcast? Why so disturbed within me? Put your hope in God, for I will yet praise him, my Savior and my God."

Remember, you are more precious than diamonds—too precious to live with depression. Don't hesitate to get professional help. Follow the psalmist's six-step treatment and let God fill your heart with His peace.

Cry **from my Heart** | *Okay, I admit it—today I'm in a slump, Lord. But in spite of my feelings, I will determine to praise You— starting right now.*

His Proximity in Trouble
He Will Never Leave You; He Will Always Love You

One of the ways we know we are precious to the Lord is that He has committed Himself to be with us—always—and help us carry the load life has put on us. Jesus said, "Never will I leave you; never will I forsake you" (Hebrews 13:5). You would never make such a commitment to someone you didn't care about very deeply.

Yet when God allows periods of pain and hardship in our lives, we begin to wonder if He really cares. Cancer strikes—even though you've been taking care of your body. Or your home is flooded—and there's no money for repairs. Or you lose your job—just when your son is ready to start college, and now there's no money for tuition. We reason, *More precious than diamonds? I don't think so. Perhaps among all the billions of people in the world He has to keep track of, He has forgotten me—or worse yet, forsaken me.*

That's exactly how the children of Israel felt in Bible days. They declared, "The LORD has forsaken me, the Lord has forgotten me" (Isaiah 49:14). With our human limitations, perhaps that is the only way we can explain to ourselves why God doesn't rescue us immediately when we're in trouble. After all, we know He is almighty. So if we don't sense He is present with us, and we don't see Him saving us from our dilemma, we just assume He must have forgotten us and given up on us.

What does God say in reply when we feel this way? "Can a mother forget the baby at her breast and have no compassion on the child she has borne? Though she may forget, I will not forget you!" (Isaiah 49:15).

What a comparison! No mother ever forgets the child she has borne, even those who have given up their babies for adoption. Even those who have aborted babies in the earliest months of pregnancy never forget. Yet God says though a mother would forget her newborn child, "I will not forget you"! What a strong picture of His love!

And then He adds one phrase for emphasis: "See, I have engraved you on the palms of my hands" (verse 16). When I was in elementary school, when a girl had a crush on a boy, she would write his initials on her hands, such as "DD + HS." It was a semi-secret way of identifying with him.

But God in the person of Jesus Christ has more than our initials written on His hands. He has nail prints to prove His love! He suffered far more than the pangs of childbirth to make us His children. His pain was the pain of death on a cross, and His love left scars that are a reminder forever of how much He cares.

Dear precious friend, you can be sure that the One who died for you will never forget you or forsake you. Never!

Now, here's the problem. I always want to *understand* what is happening in my life. I can put up with a lot of discomfort and even misery if I know *why*. Gideon, one of the Old Testament judges, felt that way.

One day the angel of the Lord appeared to Gideon and said, "The LORD is with you, mighty warrior." Gideon responded, "Pardon me, my lord . . . but if the LORD is with us, why has all this happened to us? Where are all his wonders that our ancestors told us about when they said, 'Did not the LORD bring us up out of Egypt?' But now the LORD has abandoned us and given us into the hand of Midian" (Judges 6:12–13).

I can relate to Gideon's question. Yes, I know in my head that God has promised never to leave me or forsake me. But if that is true— and it is—why am I having such a hard time? As Gideon put it, "Why then has all this happened to us?"

God never answered the "why" question for Gideon. Instead, He gave Gideon a mission to save his people from the Midianites, who were about to attack Israel. And then He gave him a promise: "I will be with you."

The lesson of Gideon illustrates that when "all this" happens, it doesn't mean that God does not love us or has forsaken us. In fact, that may be the very time He has a mission for us, something special He wants to do through our lives. The truth that will get us through those times is that He will be with us—no matter what.

Here's what happens to me, though. When things aren't going my way and I don't understand, I begin to be anxious. Fear grips my heart.

John writes something that sounds very profound, but I had to mull it over for a while to appreciate its full meaning. He says, "Perfect love drives out fear" (1 John 4:18). No, John, I think you have it wrong. That should read, "Perfect *understanding* drives out fear." If God would just tell me *why* I have to deal with this nasty situation, I wouldn't be afraid. But that's not what John says. He says that perfect love drives out fear—that love is the supreme weapon against fear.

When I truly understand how much God loves me, it's true that fear leaves my heart like darkness flees when the sun rises. The One who loves me that much will never abandon me.

The best thing I can know during a difficult time is that the One who allows difficulty is the One who loves me more than anyone else in the whole world. No, I may not understand, but I know He loves me—deeply.

"And so we know and rely on the love God has for us. God is love" (1 John 4:16). To rely means "to believe, to commit, to put trust in."

You and I need to rest in the arms of His love. Even in painful times!

The dimensions of God's love

How big is God's love? What are its dimensions? Psalm 103 says, "As high as the heavens are above the earth, so great is his love for those who fear him. . . . From everlasting to everlasting the LORD's love is with those who fear him" (verses 11, 17).

Back up a minute and look at those dimensions of God's love—"high as the heavens" and "from everlasting to everlasting"! Scientists tell us the universe is still expanding. But never will it reach the point where God's love ends. " 'Though the mountains be shaken and the hills be removed, yet my unfailing love for you will not be shaken . . .' says the LORD" (Isaiah 54:10).

Anyone who had ever seen Mount Pinatubo, north of Manila, Philippines, before the 1990s would have said it looked permanent. Yet in June of 1991, this volcano began to erupt and spew volcanic substance for miles around. The resulting smoke cloud rose thirty-five kilometers in the air, and 78,000 people were evacuated from the surrounding area. The new summit elevation of Mount Pinatubo is 150 meters, or 500 feet lower than it was before the eruption. Thousands of tons of ash reached the upper atmosphere and changed the weather patterns of the entire world for months to come. What had looked so permanent was forever changed.

Every earthquake, every volcano is a reminder that even though mountains are not everlasting, God's love for us is! Everything that looks so permanent in your life may one day be forever changed, but God's love for you will never change.

The Apostle Paul prayed for believers going through hard times: "That you, being rooted and established in love, may have power . . . to grasp how wide and long and high and deep is the love of Christ, and to know this love that surpasses knowledge" (Ephesians 3:17–19).

I'm not quite sure how you know something that surpasses knowledge, but I think Paul meant that no matter how deeply we probe God's love, we will never reach the end of it. We can investigate it, delve into its depths, and explore its reach, but we will never come to the end of God's love. Corrie ten Boom said, "There is no pit so deep, that God's love is not deeper still."

"For I am convinced," wrote Paul, "that neither death nor life, neither angels nor demons, neither the present nor the future, neither lack of money nor problems in the family, neither super-typhoons nor illness, nor any powers, neither height nor depth, nor anything else in all creation, will be able to separate us from the love of God that is in Christ Jesus our Lord" (Romans 8:38–39, *my paraphrase*).

So what does that mean in my life? It means I can truly rest in His love for me. I can relax in the recliner of His love. Yes, I can close my eyes, lean back, and know that though everything I count on in life may fail, God's love will never fail.

Now what are you going to do with that load of cares you've been carrying? The psalmist said, "Cast your cares on the LORD and he will sustain you" (Psalm 55:22). It's a verse that always challenges me. I think that's because I've always taken responsibility very seriously. I find it very easy to get uptight. I tend to carry around a big load of cares. I make lists of them—on my Mac, on my iPhone, and on various pieces of paper. *Family Circle* magazine had a term for people like me: "listomaniacs."

Why do I carry my cares around when God says to cast them on Him? I believe there are a number of reasons—I thought of five:

1   I think to myself, *This problem is my responsibility, so I'd better be the one to take care of it.*

2   When I worry, I feel like I'm at least doing *something* about the problem.

3   Maybe I can fix it myself—and faster than God would do it.

4   I'm not sure He'll fix it the way I want it fixed.

5   It's scary to let it go.

Do any of those reasons sound familiar to you? Turn to God, who says, "Cast all your care on Me." That's different than saying, "Don't worry, be happy." He's not saying, "Just forget about your problems." He's saying, "Put them on Me! I have broad shoulders. No problem is too big for Me to carry."

There's a verse in Hebrews that says, "Do not cast away your confidence, which has great reward" (Hebrews 10:35 NKJV). God says, "Don't cast away your confidence, but instead cast your cares—on Me." But what do we do? We get it backwards. We cast away our *confidence* and carry our *cares*!

Sometimes I need to be told I'm taking too much responsibility—more than God intended. He knows I'm not strong enough to carry around my cares and carry out my responsibilities at the same time. He knows I'll get discouraged and want to give up. So He gives me a solution:

My part: Cast my cares on Him.

His part: Sustain me.

It's easy to say you believe this, but this is a truth that can change your entire attitude if you will absorb it into your life. Will you cast your cares on Him right now?

Cry from my Heart

*I've decided, Lord,
to lean hard on You today.
I know You're with me.
Hold me close.*

His Path to Contentment—
An Impossible Dream?

Our hostess in the Philippines was treating us to two days outside of Manila, a welcome change from crowds and concrete. We had spent the first day shooting the rapids at Pagsanjan Falls in Laguna, and now we were settling into a little cottage beside a beautiful lake, chosen especially for Harold and me because it was the only cottage with a "heater." I had thought, *Why would we want a heater in the tropics? Oh, I get it—a water heater!* I'll admit the idea of a warm shower was appealing.

Yes, the cottage had a shower. But the shower stall also had a large bucket of water and a little dipper. In this country, it doesn't take long for you to realize that this arrangement is very handy when the water supply gives out just after you have lathered up.

The next thing I learned about the bathroom was that the toilet didn't flush. After Harold had worked on it for a while, he asked one of our staff members to report the problem to the resort office. In the meantime, I decided to go ahead and turn on the shower so the water could warm up. Good idea. Except there wasn't enough water pressure to make the system work. Plan B: Fill the bucket with warm water. Remember the dipper? I got exactly one dipper-full of warm water before the temperature turned cold again. So I set that warm water aside for rinsing my hair.

But at that precise moment, the guys came to work on the toilet, so I exited the bathroom. Do you know what they did with my one dipper of warm water? They poured it into the toilet!

When the men finished, it was dinnertime and so I could not take my shower. And by the time the late dinner was over, I was too tired to face cold water. (By the way, the toilet still didn't flush!) I washed a bit and climbed into bed—still sticky.

Harold climbed into bed, too—and then he had the audacity to ask me, "Do you want to pray?"

"No!" I said, quite firmly.

The next morning I woke up early for my cold dipper-shower, only to discover that the banana I had left on a table across the room was now lying on the floor beside the bed. Thank God I never saw the rat, but I knew he had been there!

Then I thought of the verse in Philippians that says, "I have learned to be content whatever the circumstances" (Philippians 4:11). Not me! I have been involved in Christian work, much of it overseas, for more than fifty years. Yet I have so much to learn!

Contentment! What does it take to make you content? Great possessions? Great circumstances? Or at least a warm shower?

I admit I'm somewhat of a Home and Garden Television addict. Well, maybe not an addict, but definitely a fan! For a while there was a program on our HGTV channel called *I Want That!* On this show were featured the newest gadgets and latest gizmos. I had once thought to myself, *Those producers have latched on to a very human trait. We all want the latest and best, whether needed or not.*

I was reminded of what Richard Foster wrote in his challenging book *Freedom of Simplicity*:

> We are told by television that the most idiotic things will make us insanely happy. The purpose of all this media bombardment is to increase desire. The plan is to change "That's extravagant" into "That would be nice to have," and then into "I really need that," and finally into "I've got to have it!"[37]

Never mind that we are precious to God, that we have countless promises of His provision and care. Like Eve, who saw the beautiful fruit, we're quick to say, "I want that!"

Even the Apostle Paul may have struggled with covetousness. (Covetousness? Oh yes, that's what it is. We might as well call it by its correct name.) Paul wrote, "I would not have known what coveting really was if the law had not said, 'You shall not covet.' But sin, seizing an opportunity afforded by the commandment, produced in me every kind of coveting" (Romans 7:7–8). Paul, too, was tempted with wanting what he didn't have. But Scripture so clearly reminds us: "Be content with what you have" (Hebrews 13:5).

So, what is the answer? Give everything away? Is being poor the answer to living a contented life? Not necessarily. Foster went on to say, "Poverty is not simplicity. It is quite possible to get rid of things and still desire them in your heart."[38]

The Apostle Paul, however, must have conquered his struggle, for he later wrote that verse I quoted at the beginning of this chapter, "I have learned to be content whatever the circumstances" (Philippians 4:11). He certainly didn't say it because his circumstances were easy:

> I have worked much harder, been in prison more frequently, been flogged more severely, and been exposed to death again and again. Five times I received from the Jews the forty lashes minus one. Three times I was beaten with rods, once I was stoned, three times I was shipwrecked, I spent a night and a day in the open sea, I have been constantly on the move. I have been in danger from rivers, in danger from bandits, in danger from my own countrymen, in danger from Gentiles; in danger in the city, in danger in the country, in danger at sea; and in danger

> from false brothers. I have labored and
> toiled and have often gone without
> sleep; I have known hunger and thirst
> and have often gone without food;
> I have been cold and naked.
> (*2 Corinthians 11:23–27*)

How could Paul, after what he had been through, be content? Obviously, his contentment had little to do with his circumstances. I believe we find the answer when Paul says he had a "thorn in the flesh" that God chose not to remove. He told Paul, "My grace is sufficient for you" (2 Corinthians 12:9). Do we really believe that?

To make this easier to remember, I'd like to give you five practical suggestions for content-ment that are an acrostic of the word GRACE.

G — Be Grateful

Colossians 3:16 talks about having "gratitude in your hearts." When we compare ourselves to those who have more than we do, we rob ourselves of contentment. When we compare ourselves to those who have less than we do, our hearts are filled with gratitude. You've probably heard the saying, "I complained because I had no shoes—until I met a man who had no feet."

All right, let's make this practical right where we live. Let me ask you, is there anything you would like to change, for example, about the house you live in? I'm sure I can hear you answering, "Yes! I'd like a new sofa and a new refrigerator and—well, the list goes on and on."

On several trips to Africa, I have visited the Maasai people, who live in kraals, huts made of rough-cut mud-plastered branches, surrounded by a fence of thorn bushes. The dirt floors of the huts are coated with dung that keeps down the flea population. Children grow up walking bare-foot on mud and cow dung, their snotty noses and runny eyes collecting flies. On my first trip to Kenya, I overheard an American lady say to her friend, "Slap me if I ever complain about anything again!" We are soooo rich! I say this not to make us feel guilty but grateful.

We live in nice houses with comfortable beds. We eat in nice restaurants and attend lovely churches. Yet many of us would admit we're not content. For we must still deal with serious problems—marriage conflicts, children who make bad decisions and bring us heartache, life-threatening diseases, grief over the loss of loved ones, and feeling overwhelmed with life's responsibilities.

In Ann Voskamp's *New York Times* best-seller *One Thousand Gifts*, she starts by telling that when she was four, her next-younger sister was crushed under the wheels of a truck in front of their house while their mother looked on in horror. She also had a baby sister who was only three weeks old at the time. The trauma was so great that her mother ended up spending weeks in a psych ward. Financial problems set in. A box of macaroni and cheese would be shared by four people—and even at that, half was saved for another meal. By the time Ann was seven, she had developed an ulcer. Panic attacks set in at age twenty. Ann wrote of that time:

> How do I fully live when life is full of hurt? How do I wake up to joy and grace and beauty and all that is the fullest life when I must stay numb to losses and crushed dreams and all that empties me out?[39]

For years of mornings, she woke up wanting to die.

> I wake to self-hatred. To the wrestle to get it all done, the relentless anxiety that I am failing. . . . I yell at children, fester with bitterness, forget doctor

> appointments, lose library books, live
> selfishly, skip prayer, complain, go
> to bed too late, neglect cleaning the
> toilets. I live tired. Afraid. Anxious.
> Weary.[40]

Then a friend dared Ann to make a list of a
thousand things she was thankful for. A thousand! Quite an assignment! So Ann kept note-
books open in various parts of the house where,
between caring for and homeschooling her six
children, she'd write down things like mail in
the mailbox, warm cookies, clean sheets smell-
ing like the wind, hair bows holding back curls,
forgiveness of a sister, toothless smiles, a child's
sobs ebbing, laughter at twilight, book pages
turning, the glow of the front porch light.

Big things? Seldom. But all just small gifts
God had given her that she never had eyes to
see before because she was too busy rushing on
to the next thing she had to do. And what was
the result? Ann's attitude began to change. She
wasn't so quick to be angry. Acknowledging
God's small gifts, she began to see His hand in
the difficulties as well as the blessings. She could
trust Him more readily. Not only did contentment fill her life, but pure *joy* began to fill
her heart!

Right now, I'm going to challenge you to do the same thing—like Ann, begin your list of one thousand gifts God has given you. You'll need a notebook or a file on your computer or cell phone. If every day you jotted down three things, by the end of the year you will have a list of one thousand gifts.

Ephesians 5:20 speaks of "*always* giving thanks *for all* things in the name of our Lord Jesus Christ" (NASB, italics mine). It's easy to say, "I'm thankful for everything." It's totally different to make a list of God's gifts to you. Doing this will change your life.

R— Rest in His promises

"[God] has given us his very great and precious promises, so that through them you may participate in the divine nature, having escaped the corruption in the world caused by evil desires" (2 Peter 1:4). God's promises help us to be more like Him and to escape covetousness—or any other sin we're dealing with.

Armin Gesswein was a twenty-four-year-old Lutheran pastor striving to plant a church on Long Island, New York, and things were not going well. In his church fellowship was a retired blacksmith, Ambrose Whaley, about fifty years his senior. Armin had noticed that when this man prayed, things happened. "The prayer and the answer were not far apart," Armin used to tell us. "In fact, they were moving along together. Uncle Am's 'prayer muscles' were extremely strong because of much exercise." Wanting to learn his spiritual secrets, Armin asked if he might join the old blacksmith in prayer.

At the blacksmith's home, they went to the barn and climbed up into the hayloft. Armin prayed. Then the old blacksmith prayed. Finally Armin turned to Ambrose and said, "You have some kind of a secret in praying. Would you mind sharing it with me?"

"Young man," said the blacksmith, "learn to plead the promises of God." The old man had knelt between two bales of hay, and on each bale was an open Bible. His large hands, gnarled and toughened by years of hard labor, were open, covering the pages of each Bible.

Armin told us, "I learned more about prayer in that haymow than in all my years of schooling for the ministry."

My favorite promise concerning prayer is 1 John 5:14–15: "This is the confidence we have in approaching God: that if we ask anything according to his will, he hears us. And if we know that he hears us—whatever we ask—we know that we have what we asked of him."

How straightforward is that! Settle it once and for all: God's promises are trustworthy!

You can rest in them.

A – Accept the circumstances

"LORD, you alone are my portion and my cup" (Psalm 16:5). Kim Thomas, in her book *Even God Rested,* speaks of everyday irritations that push her to her limits:

> I find people with too many items in
> the fast-checkout line at the store, and
> elevators that don't come when called,
> and . . . people who cancel plans at the
> last minute, and store clerks who know
> nothing about the products they sell,
> and . . . people who don't respect the
> rules about swimming laps in their own
> lanes at the pool and the lifeguards
> who do nothing about it, and . . . cars
> that are out of gas when I am in a hurry
> . . . and things in general not going the
> way I expected are some of the things
> that send me falling down into a fit
> of anger.[41]

It doesn't take much to make us discontented.

But perhaps you'd be thrilled if these kinds of things were the only difficult situations you'd have to deal with. Some of you have circumstances that are almost unbearable: a child with a terminal illness, a husband who is cheating on you, a parent with mental illness, whose care you are responsible for, tremendous debt that was not your fault . . . and on and on. Can God help you accept *those* circumstances?

Cynthia Heald writes that she will never forget the summer her family moved to Temple, Texas. She had three children under the age of three. Her husband, Jack, was a busy veterinarian—rarely at home. She says it was a good thing they lived next door to the animal clinic and could go next door anytime they wanted to remember what he looked like!

Cynthia soon learned that cows that had difficulty calving did so just as Jack sat down to a meal with the family. Her next lesson was that her children were not the only ones blessed with living next door to the clinic. It was very convenient for the local rats that ate at the clinic and nested in their house. One day the reality hit her that she was running a bed-and-breakfast for rats! She spent the summer of 1965 with rats running up and down the walls, cooking in a kitchen with one small sink flanked by a scant foot of counter on either side, an absent husband, two babies in diapers, a newborn who wasn't sleeping, and no close friends. She was ready to resign!

One afternoon Cynthia went to her room, stretched out across her bed, and cried out to God, "I give up! I'm so tired of trying to live life in my own strength."

"Good, Cynthia," she heard God say in her heart. *"I've been waiting for you to give up."*

She then remembered she had once heard a preacher say that when you are born, you are given a car to drive on the highway of life. At twelve, Cynthia had stopped and invited Jesus Christ into her life. But then she put Him in the backseat and kept driving. Now at twenty-six, she felt His tap on her shoulder to "move over" and let Him take the steering wheel. That afternoon she signed up for the whole tour: the itinerary was His, the lodging was *definitely* His, her family, routine, and the rats—all His.

She said an amazing thing happened. Not one part of her life changed outwardly. She still lived in an old house for four more years, still had three small, needy children, and Jack was as busy as ever. But inwardly, there was a change. She saw things differently. She put it this way:

> I no longer owned my life.[42] . . . I accepted the Lord's invitation to wear His yoke the afternoon I relinquished control of my life. None of the circumstances of my life changed, but I immediately began to experience His rest. Because of this rest, I knew I could continue with my life as it was. I also began to know the Lord's guidance and instruction in fresh ways. I was more attentive to the Scriptures and to His voice because I had put on His yoke.[43]

Maybe this is your time to give up, to move over, and to let God take the steering wheel of your life.

C — remember that your Citizenship is in heaven

"But our citizenship is in heaven. And we eagerly await a Savior from there, the Lord Jesus Christ" (Philippians 3:20).

When Paul wrote to the Philippians, Philippi, the capital of Macedonia (northern Greece), was a Roman colony. Roman citizenship had been granted to the citizens as a special favor. It was a great privilege that enabled each Philippian, though living in Macedonia, to say proudly, "My citizenship is in Rome." His responsibilities were directly to the emperor in Rome, not to the provincial government of Macedonia.

Similarly to the Philippians, our citizenship is not here on earth—it is in heaven. God has given us heavenly citizenship. Our primary allegiance is to God. And He is responsible for us. This life is temporary. As Tim LaHaye says,

> "For the Christian, this life is as bad as it gets."

What an encouragement!

> For the Lord himself will come down from heaven, with a loud command, with the voice of the archangel and with the trumpet call of God, and the dead in Christ will rise first. After that, we who are still alive and are left will be caught up together with them in the clouds to meet the Lord in the air. And so we will be with the Lord forever. Therefore encourage one another with these words. *(1 Thessalonians 4:16–18)*

$\mathcal{E}$ — realize God is Enough

Money is the root of all evil, right? Wrong! *Love* of money is the problem (see 1 Timothy 6:10). Paul had conquered that problem, for he wrote, "I know what it is to be in need, and I know what it is to have plenty. I have learned the secret of being content in any and every situation, whether well fed or hungry, whether living in plenty or in want" (Philippians 4:12). The King James Version puts it this way: "I know both how to be abased, and I know how to abound."

We think a lot about how to be content when *abased*, but do you ever think about how to *abound*? I once read that people in the US living below poverty level are still in the top six percent of the world's economy. In America, at least, we need to think, "How should I handle my riches?"

My neighbor Terri and I were walking together early one morning just after I had returned from a ministry trip overseas. She made me pause in my tracks when she asked, "How do you travel overseas and see what you do and come home and live where we do?" Granted, we both live in nice houses and we are both concerned about missions.

The secret is this: It all belongs to the Lord—not 10 percent His (the tithe) and 90 percent mine to spend as I please, but 100 percent His to use as He wishes.

When Bill and Vonette Bright, founders of Campus Crusade for Christ, were newlyweds, they made sure to set priorities for their lives. After making a list of everything they owned, including their brand-new wedding gifts, they drew up a legal document and signed over the ownership of everything to God. When they gave everything to God, they found that He is enough.

No, contentment is *not* an impossible dream. We can find God's GRACE to be content where He has put us if only we will

Be **G**rateful
Rest in His promises
Accept the circumstances
Remember that our **C**itizenship is in heaven
Realize that God is **E**nough

Now, God doesn't say, "Shut up and be content." If you still want or need more than you have, the Bible gives us the solution—it's prayer. "Do not be anxious about anything, but in every situation, by prayer and petition, with thanksgiving, present your requests to God. And the peace of God, which transcends all understanding, will guard your hearts and your minds in Christ Jesus" (Philippians 4:6–7).

Cry from my **Heart** | *Lord, I confess I'm not content with some of the circumstances in my life. I really want them changed right now! Give me Your grace to wait for Your timing.*

His Privileged Relationship—
Intimacy with God

Awhile back, I was going through one of those times when I was dissatisfied with my relationship with the Lord. Oh, I was doing "okay"—that is, I wasn't consciously sinning. But to tell you the truth, I was bored. Everything seemed mechanical—not at all intimate.

I was especially dissatisfied with my prayer time—which was about as exciting as repeating a grocery list. "Lord, You know everything on the list anyway—it's a waste of time for both of us for me to mention these needs to You every day."

I told the Lord I loved Him. I praised and thanked Him. But what was missing was a truly intimate time with God, where I "crawled up into His arms," shared the deepest feelings of my heart—including the not-so-nice parts—and then just listened.

At about this time I received a little book by Jill Briscoe called *The Garden of Grace*. In this book, Jill pictures herself sitting on steps leading to a lovely garden and meeting God there. The first line says: "Something happens when your soul sits down and has a rest."[44] My attention was captured. My soul was so tired! I desperately needed to sit down with God and just rest.

Jill said that as she sat quietly with her Bible, God began to read the Bible to her, and it was as if she were reading it for the very first time. Truths previously read in a hurry began to glow. The Bible became her Golden Book. Time and time again I have needed to come back to this relationship with God.

I have become more and more impressed that God wants an intimate connection with each of us. And I believe you, too, may be heart-hungry for this kind of relationship. When we know Jesus as our Savior, God calls Himself our Father and us His children. Jesus says He is our elder Brother. Most intimate of all, Jesus pictures Himself as a Groom and us as His bride. Marriage is the closest of all human relationships. Can you believe He wants that warm, cherished, intimate relationship with *us*? We may know it theoretically, but do we experience it? As Dr. Joseph Stowell writes, "Intimacy is fanned when there is nothing more important to me than my deepening relationship with the one that I love. It works this way in marriage. It works this way with God."[45]

Expressing our love to God

Author and counselor Dr. Gary Chapman says that human beings have five love languages—that is, ways we communicate love: acts of service, touch, gifts, words of affirmation, and quality time. Do you know what your love language is? In what way do you like someone to express love to you?

- by kind things they do for you?

- by reaching for your hand or giving you a hug?

- by giving you a gift?

- by the kind words they say to you?

- by doing something with you that you like to do?

I believe we can express our love to God in these five love languages as well:

- **Acts of service:** This might be driving for someone, running errands, cooking for a neighbor, or teaching a class for

a friend when she's ill. The Bible says,
"So whether you eat or drink or what-
ever you do, do it all for the glory of
God" (1 Corinthians 10:31).

❀ **Touch**: not physical but emotional closeness—touching God in prayer as we
spend intimate time in His presence.

❀ **Gifts**: sacrificial offerings we give
because we love Him.

❀ **Words of praise and thanksgiving**: The
Bible talks about a sacrifice of praise.

❀ And probably the most valuable: **quality
time**

I'd like to say more about that last one. There's
almost nothing we can give God that He doesn't
already own—nothing we can tell Him that He
does not already know. The one thing we can
give to God, however, is our time—quality time
with Him. We all have the same amount of time:
168 hours a week, 24 hours a day. We decide
how we are going to use that time. Some needs
to be spent just sitting quietly with God. Psalm
46:10 says, "Be still, and know that I am God."

But it's so hard to be still. There's an old
hymn that says, "I'll live for Him who died

for me." Actually, here's what I've discovered: I'll work for Him, organize, give, teach, etc.— usually anything but *be still*. Yet deep, intimate fellowship with Him is, I believe, what His heart longs for and actually one of the few things I can give to God that He wants.

Satan's desire is to keep us away from communion with God.

He doesn't care how he deters us from that intimate closeness, but in my experience I've seen Satan do it three ways:

1   He keeps us busy.

Someone said that if Satan can't get us to sin, he'll just let us work ourselves to death. I am very vulnerable to that. I can identify with Jill Briscoe when she tells of a time she found herself running on empty. She had given and given and given until she simply had nothing left to give.

> "Maybe I need to stop running," she said to God. "All this activity—my Sunday school class, take a break from youth work—just stay home and regroup."
> "You mean quit?" [God said to her]
> "No, but maybe I should stop running so fast and furious."

> "You don't need to stop running,
> Jill, you need to stop running on
> empty!"[46]

Today, every woman is a busy woman. Sometimes the mornings are so busy you have no time
for breakfast. Then you grab a piece of fruit
and maybe a bag of chips for lunch. Come 4
p.m., you wonder why you're so exhausted. The
answer is obvious—lack of nutrition. But don't
you and I do exactly the same when it comes
to spiritual food—and then we wonder why we
have no spiritual strength. It's because we're
trying to run on empty.

Jill adds, "I've found that the devil never
stops trying to get us running on empty one way
or another. Don't let him do it to you! Go to the
Deep Place inside you: you'll find Him waiting.
He'll say to your soul, 'The journey is too great
for you, rest here awhile. Let me prepare some
food for your soul. We'll eat together.'"[47]

2   **Satan tries to keep us from deep commu-
    nion with God by sending so much trouble
    that we doubt God's love.**
When this happens, it's time for us to get a new
perspective on God. And the way that works
best for me is to take a fresh look at the universe

God has created. I'm blown away by the sheer size of it. Science tells us the farthest object we can see in the universe is perhaps ten billion light-years away. But since I don't really grasp what even one light-year is, let alone ten billion, this truth needs to be broken down to facts I can comprehend.

So let's look at it this way. If the thickness of a piece of paper represents the distance from the earth to the sun, the distance to the next nearest star would be the thickness of a seventy-one-foot-high stack of paper. The distance across our own galaxy would be represented by a stack 310 miles high, while the edge of the known universe would not be reached until you had a pile of paper thirty-one million miles high. Now that's a very big stack of paper![48]

But the truth of the matter is that I know the One who made all that. He's my Shepherd. This is what He says, "My own hand laid the foundations of the earth, and my right hand spread out the heavens" (Isaiah 48:13). And I have a relationship with that great Creator God.

At Guidelines we receive e-mails and messages from people going through difficult circumstances: "Why does God do this to me?" As believers, all that is allowed into our lives is filtered through His hands for the purpose of working out good. Not all that happens *is* good, but He can use it to work *for* our good. If we have strayed from Him or simply don't feel close to Him, perhaps He has allowed problems to come to drive us back to Himself. God wants a close relationship with us even if He has to use trouble to bring us to that kind of bonding.

God takes note of the smallest seed and tiniest sparrow. He is not too busy to keep records even of my falling hair. Psalm 56:8 says, "You have recorded my troubles. You have kept a list of my tears. Aren't they in your records?" (Psalm 56:8 NCV). Yet when we're in the middle of a problem, we suppose He has overlooked us. He hasn't. He just wants to draws us closer to Himself. Confucius says that a diamond "cannot be polished without friction, nor the man perfected without trials." Faith is even more precious, so faith will always be tested.

If there is one truth in the universe you must hold on to through these tests, it's that God loves you. You may not understand it, but that truth never changes. God may allow pain and suffering, but the One who gave His Son for you never stops caring.

3   Satan tries to disrupt our communion with God by sending just enough money that we think we don't need God.

Remember when Jesus told the story of the man sowing seed in Matthew 13? Some of the seed (which represents the Word of God) fell on thorny ground, where spiky plants grew up and choked the tender seedlings. One of the thorns mentioned was the "deceitfulness of riches." You say, "Well, I'm certainly not rich, so that's not my problem." But riches are relative. The issue is not how much or how little we have. I have discovered that when we have enough money to meet our needs—however little or much that is—we think we don't need God.

A little boy was climbing into bed one night. His mother asked him if he had said his prayers. He replied, "No, I didn't need anything tonight." Do you and I still pray if we don't need anything? Perhaps that's why God allows need in our lives—to keep us close to Him.

How do we get this intimate relationship with God?

Of course, this close connection with God begins with our salvation, but it doesn't stop there. One day when I was reading Galatians 3, verses 2 and 3 suddenly stood out to me, as if a spotlight were shining on them:

> I would like to learn just one thing from you: Did you receive the Spirit by the works of the law, or by believing what you heard? Are you so foolish? After beginning by means of the Spirit, are you now trying to finish by means of the flesh?

Yes, Lord, as a matter of fact, I am. You saved me by grace through faith. But isn't it my responsibility to live as good a Christian life as I can?

That's what the Galatian Christians thought. They were trying to live the Christian life by their own efforts. Some may actually have been in Jerusalem at Pentecost and received the Holy Spirit there, so they knew it wasn't by obeying Jewish laws that they had received God's Spirit. Paul stressed that just as they had begun their Christian lives in the power of the Spirit, so they should grow by the Spirit's power. We must realize that we grow spiritually because of God's work in us by His Spirit, not by following special rules or by our own efforts.

The Ten Commandments aren't the only mandates given to us in the Bible. There are far more than ten—commands like

* love one another (John 13:34);

* forgive as the Lord forgave you (Colossians 3:13);

* pray continually (1 Thessalonians 5:17).

I'm the first to admit I can't consistently do *any* of these with human effort. It's impossible.

Take, for instance, the command to love our enemies (Matthew 5:44). One day my husband and I were riding in a New York City taxi on our way to the airport. Conversation with our taxi driver made us wonder at first if he might be a Christian, but after a minute or so, we realized he was a Muslim, and the topic of discussion turned to relations between Christians and Muslims. Our driver admitted that we needed to get along with one another. My husband quoted Jesus' command to love our enemies. Instantly the driver snapped, "That's impossible!" In a sense, he was right. You and I can't love our enemies with our own love. We need the power of God's Spirit to obey that command. So what makes us think we can live *any* of the Christian life with our own abilities in our own power? Jesus Himself told us, "Apart from me you can do nothing" (John 15:5).

God has given us spiritual disciplines and practices by which we grow in intimacy with Him and bring Him glory—you know, read your Bible every day, pray, attend church, share your faith. These are worthy pursuits. But when the Christian life becomes regulation-driven rather than heartthrob-powered by the Holy Spirit, nothing spiritual happens.

Look at it this way: If your own children did what you told them to do but spent as little time as possible with you and never gave you a hug or told you they loved you, they'd still be your kids, but you wouldn't have much of a relationship. Stop right there for a moment. Do you ever give God a hug? Do you tell Him every day that you love Him—the words He longs to hear?

A lot of people think that in order to please God, we need to intensify our efforts at Bible study, Scripture memory, and working for Him. But that won't work—it will only make us tired.

Some of us are afraid of a closer relationship with God because we figure He's going to demand more and more from us. So we avoid getting too close to Him for fear He'll add to the load we're already carrying. After all, everything in us cries out to lay our burdens down, not take on more. I believe Bruce Wilkinson has the answer when he advises, "Do less *for* God . . . be more *with* God."[49] Nothing will substitute for time spent with God, sharing from the depths of our hearts and listening to His.

We all run tired. That's why we need to run to the Lord every time our peace is disturbed. He is the source of true rest. "Come to Me," He calls to us. Deep inside, we know we need quiet time to hear God speak to us. Deep inside, we know He is the only source of strength. Psalm 73:26 says, "My flesh and my heart may fail, but God is the strength of my heart and my portion forever." Chuck Swindoll says, "There's something about slowing down, shutting up, and listening that prompts the Holy Spirit to speak."[50]

C. S. Lewis, who was born in 1898, tells us how *not* to have that kind of relationship: "Avoid silence, avoid solitude. Keep the radio on."[51] Just imagine what he would add to that list today—TV, cell phones, Facebook, Twitter, video games, to name just a few.

Maybe you're thinking, "Sitting quietly isn't my style. There's nothing quiet about me. I'm an outspoken type-A person. I'm never still. That verse that says Christian women are to have a gentle and quiet spirit [1 Peter 3:4]—that one makes me uncomfortable."

That verse doesn't say you must have a "quiet personality." I've met women who were very quiet but ruled their households with emotional blackmail. No one wanted to cross them because they could easily dissolve into tears and make living with them very difficult. God made each of us with a unique personality, which is what makes getting to know one another so interesting. He wants us to be ourselves, not like someone else.

The word "quiet" describes the kind of spirit we're to have as godly women: "a tranquility arising from within, causing no disturbance to others."[52] I suspect your family would like *that*!

But what about on mornings when everybody has woken up late? Your husband yells, "Where are my socks?" You hear your daughter's voice, "Mom, I can't find my sweater." Your son brings his favorite T-shirt to you: "My shirt has a big hole in it! And where's my report? I'm late!" Sometimes you feel like locking yourself in the bathroom just to get some peace and quiet. And don't think that getting in the car and driving to work will help on a day like this, because you will probably have forgotten to get gas and be even later!

Do you have a quiet spirit when all that happens? Probably not. But some quiet time might help. Maybe not two hours, but just two minutes. Take a quick look in your Promise Book, grab a verse you've marked in your Bible, send a quick SOS prayer to the Lord—and hold on to Him with all your might until you can find a quiet spot for more concentrated communication with Him.

There are many ways to express the idea of intimacy with God. My friend Vicki calls it *becoming attached to God*. She is a physician who as a believer has searched for life in all its fullness. Over the years, she has shared her frustration in finding the answer she has been looking for. But her last e-mail told me she was getting close. Vicki said she has given up demanding that life must "work out" as she thinks it should. "My goal and desire is to become more and more attached to God," she says. "It is *not* taking a vacation from the realness of life at all, just embracing both the blessings and the heartaches." She has given up trying to find the formula for "success" as a Christian. Instead, she is clinging to the One who loves her. No longer does she demand that circumstances bring her pleasure and happiness. She's becoming attached to God!

Madame Jeanne Guyon talked about *abandonment to God*. This is the French noblewoman (referred to in an earlier chapter) who lived in the 1600s, who endured a difficult marriage along with a difficult mother-in-law, and still kept communion with God. Because of her strong devotion to the Lord in the midst of political upheaval, she later ended up in the infamous Bastille prison for four years. Yet Madame Guyon wrote: "I introduce a new word to you. The word is *abandonment*. To penetrate deeper in the experience of Jesus Christ, it is required that you begin to abandon your whole existence, giving it up to God." Notice this: "You must utterly believe that the circumstances of your life, that is, every minute of your life—anything, yes, *everything* that happens—have all come to you by His will and by His permission. You must utterly believe that everything that has happened to you is from God and is exactly what you need."[53] Easy? No. But this is true abandonment to God.

Scary—the thought of giving up all control. Leaving all in God's hands. Are you ready to do that? You may be afraid to relax your grip. On the other hand, are you weary and seriously heart-hungry for God? Then you will be willing to take the challenge. The good part is that He is heart-hungry for you, too. He created us for intimacy with Him. He is after our hearts.

Conference speaker Ruth Myers said that no aspect of the love of God does more for her than the truth that He desires her. It's the picture of a groom pursuing his bride. Ruth says that, as her response, "God wants me to love Him with all of my heart." She used to be troubled by the command to love the Lord with all her heart, soul, and mind because she knew she couldn't do it. But now she considers it the most flattering verse in Scripture—that God would *want* her to love Him that way. Imagine, she says, that the most desirable boy in the class came up to you and said, "I wish you'd love me with all of your heart." You'd be thrilled! It's a compliment that God, who needs nothing, wants our love.[54]

Take time to meet Him. Take time to be filled with His Spirit. Run to Him! Sit with Him! Listen to Him! Let Him read the Bible to you. You will find new strength—new fuel—for the responsibilities He has given you. And you will have a new realization of how precious you are to Him.

Cry from my Heart	*Guard my heart today, Lord, from wanting more than I need. If I have YOU, what more could I need?*

Lord,
I'm at the end
of all my resources.

Child,
You're just at the beginning
of Mine.

— Ruth Harms Calkin
The One Year Book of Bible Promises[55]

PART THREE

Don't Waste
Your Valuable Life!

VALUE (verb)
- to estimate the monetary worth of (something)
- to consider (someone or something) to be important or beneficial; have a high opinion of

Synonyms: evaluate, assess, appraise, put/set a price on, hold in high regard, rate highly, esteem, set great store by, put stock in, appreciate, respect

What Do You Do with a Diamond?

What do you do with a diamond? Well, first you'll probably want to get it appraised so you have some idea of how valuable it is. Then you'll want to protect it and care for it. And finally, you'll want to display it appropriately in the perfect setting.

That's exactly what God has done for you, precious sister. He's told you how much you're worth—the sacrifice of His Son at Calvary. You can never do anything to go beyond that love, for God's love for you will never run out.

Then, if you read His Word, you'll see promises that He will protect you and care for you in every situation. Not that your life will necessarily be easy. We'd never grow if we only coasted downhill in life. Remember that diamonds can withstand lots of heat and pressure—and so can you if God is inside you.

As you would your diamond, God will put you on display so others can see the beauty He has created in your life. He will carefully arrange the circumstances of your life just like the carefully placed prongs of a diamond's setting, enabling the beauty deep within the stone to sparkle brilliantly. Some of the circumstances you're dealing with right now may seem very dark. But remember that a jeweler always displays his gems against black velvet to show off their brilliance.

So far in this book, we've talked about how precious you are to God—far more precious than the largest diamond ever found. No, more precious than *all* the diamonds in the world put together. And we've also talked about some of the resources God has provided for you to live a life that's in keeping with the value He places on you.

This last section is the most challenging. If we're so very valuable—and we are—then let's not waste this precious life. Let's make the very most of it. Don't worry, I don't mean that we should be busier than ever. As Mary Byers says,

> *Your busyness level does not determine your worth. Sadly, we often determine our own importance based on how busy we are and equate a demanding schedule with a meaningful life. However, there's no correlation. Being busy doesn't make you important, and a full schedule doesn't mean you're living a life of meaning and purpose. All it means is that you're busy!*[56]

John Piper wrote a book I like very much, entitled *Don't Waste Your Life*. What a great title! That's what we're striving for—living a life of meaning and purpose. I feel sure you want to make your life count for something that lasts beyond this life. Why waste the only thing that can't be replaced—the incredibly valuable gift of life God has given us? That's what we're going to look at in these final pages.

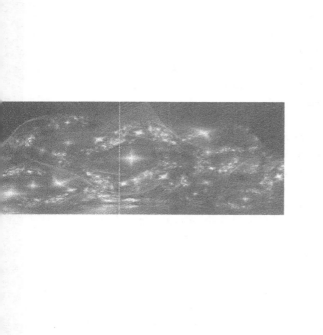

What Do You Have
A Passion For?

Deep down in every woman's heart, I believe, is the desire to make a difference in this life. Who wants to waste her life? Nobody. Ideally we'd like to find God's purpose for our existence and then accomplish what we're put on this earth to do. We want a cause to live for and long to know the reason the infinite First Cause of the universe created us. But some of us don't believe we are capable of living much beyond ourselves—we're too shy, too "dumb," too poor, too disabled, too *whatever*. Maybe your self-esteem is so low you don't feel qualified to accomplish anything meaningful. Abuse may have left its scars on your heart. Or, you may feel like you've made too many mistakes and bad choices. But I'm not talking about just *doing* something great. I'm talking about *being*

the person God created you to be. He knows you better than anyone else—your talents, your abilities, your heart desires—and your faults and failures, too. He wants to take you just as you are and work in your life in such a way that you will touch the lives of those around you.

In Proverbs 23:26 God says, "Give me your heart and let your eyes delight in my ways." If God has our hearts, He has *us*. And I want to assure you that if He has the control center of your life, you will see Him work in your life in amazing ways.

The question I'm asking you is this: What do you have a passion for? What energizes you? What do you have boundless enthusiasm for? Don't make this complicated for yourself. Just be honest. Do you love children? Like to grow organic foods? Write? Travel? Solve puzzles? Plan events? Interview people? Design? Paint or make jewelry? Cook? Organize? Start or run businesses? Teach? God can use all those abilities to impact the lives of those around you.

Passion is an intense emotion, or a compelling enthusiasm or desire for anything. The term is often applied to a feeling of unusual excitement; an admiration for a cause or activity; an *affinity* or love toward a subject or thing. That's

a long definition that you probably don't even
need, because, honestly, if you have a passion,
you just know it. When you're engaged in an
activity you're passionate about, time flies by;
the effort required seems easy. But what is *your*
passion? If you could be doing anything you
want in your life right now, what would it be?
The answer defines your passion.

Now let's relate passion to God's will for
your life. Are they identical? Well, they're certainly related. My husband says that passion is
the faint outline of God's will for you. Usually
God calls you to do something you're good at.
You may not know that you're good at it when
you first start out, but you'll find out as you
go along.

Dr. Margaret Brand was serving with her
famous hand surgeon husband, Dr. Paul Brand,
on the staff of Christian Medical College and
Hospital in Vellore, South India. She had given
birth to baby Mary just two weeks before, when
she received a note saying,

> Dear Margaret,
>   We don't wish to hurry you, but
> we must have more help in the Eye
> Department as soon as possible.

Earlier when they had asked her where she wanted to work, she had told them, "I don't mind where you put me, just as long as it isn't in the Eye Department." It was an area of medicine she knew little about that provoked fear in her heart. She now turned the piece of paper over and wrote, "Don't mind being hurried, but I know nothing about eyes. You'll have to look for someone else. Sorry . . ."

One hour later the messenger returned with another note that said, simply:

"You'll learn. Please start on Monday." She says, "Six words on a little slip of paper changed my life." The result was that Dr. Margaret served for eighteen years in India and an additional twenty-two years in Carville, Louisiana, where she was chief of Ophthalmology and an expert in leprosy of the eyes.[57]

Obviously she had a passion for medicine, but for a while God's will took her out of her comfort zone. He may do the same in your life, too.

Some of us say that we don't know what God's will for us is. So we sit around waiting for God to speak audibly, or for handwriting to appear on a wall, or for someone to walk up and say, "*This* is what God wants you to do!"

"We expect something difficult or tricky or complicated," writes Mary Byers, "so we keep looking. And we miss the very things God placed in our hearts before we were born. We look outside, hoping for divine inspiration, when in reality we should be looking inside to what we're already equipped with."[58]

I believe that usually God's will for us is in line with what He has put a passion in our hearts to do. Isn't that a great thought? In all probability, God wants you to do something you *like* to do and are good at. Something you actually consider fun!

Don't get carried away with this, however. If you're a mom and homemaker, you probably still have to scrub the toilet in your house. I've never met a person who had a passion for scrubbing toilets, but they still need to be scrubbed. But do it well, and you can at least experience the satisfaction of having the cleanest toilet in town when you're finished! God's will is for us to follow Him in the mundane as well as the spectacular.

Mary Byers talks about the "Burning Yes!" in our hearts. She writes, "A Yes! is

- something you'll do, even if you don't get paid;

- something that brings you joy;
- something that makes you lose track of time.

Usually that "Burning Yes!" causes us to touch the lives of other people, sometimes in unexpected ways.

Dr. Francis Collins is a world-renowned medical doctor and scientist who is noted for his discoveries of disease genes and his leadership of the Human Genome Project, working at the cutting edge of the study of DNA. He tells about the summer he spent in the village of Eku, Nigeria, relieving the staff physicians so that they could attend their annual conference and get a much-needed break.

Dr. Collins realized his medical skills would be pitted against unfamiliar tropical diseases and a lack of high-tech equipment. But he was not prepared for a hospital where patients often had to sleep on the floor because there were never enough beds. He says that hardest for him to accept was that the suffering he observed was in a great part due to the lack of a public health care system. The enormity of the problems, the frustration, and the exhaustion soon made him wonder why he had ever thought that a summer ⸱t there would be a good thing.

Then one afternoon, a young farmer was brought into the clinic with progressive weakness and massive swelling of his legs. His pulse practically disappeared every time he took a breath, making Dr. Collins certain the young man had accumulated a large amount of fluid in the pericardial sac around his heart. The only thing that could save him from certain death was to insert a large needle in his chest to draw off the fluid, a procedure that in the developed world would be done only by a highly trained cardiologist guided by an ultrasound machine. If the heart became lacerated, immediate death would follow.

The choice was for Dr. Collins to attempt the highly risky aspiration or watch the young man die. By now the farmer, realizing his precarious condition, calmly urged the doctor to proceed.

"With my heart in my mouth and a prayer on my lips, I inserted a large needle just under his sternum and aimed for his left shoulder. I didn't have to wait long. The rush of dark red fluid in my syringe initially made me panic that I might have entered the heart chamber, but it soon became apparent that this was . . . a massive amount of . . . effusion from the pericardial sac around the heart."[59] The young man's pulse reappeared almost immediately, and soon the swelling in his legs began to subside.

At first, relief filled Dr. Collins's heart. But by the next morning, the gloom he had felt returned, when he realized what little chance the farmer had for a long life in such a needy area of the world.

When he approached the young man's bedside, he found him reading his Bible. Sensing Dr. Collins's discouragement, the farmer spoke words that will forever be emblazoned in the doctor's mind: "I get the sense you are wondering why you came here. I have an answer for you. You came here for one reason. You came here for me." Dr. Collins reflects:

> I was stunned. Stunned that he could see so clearly into my heart, but even more stunned at the words he was speaking. I had plunged a needle close to his heart; he had directly impaled mine. With a few simple words he had put my grandiose dreams of being the great white doctor, healing the African millions, to shame. He was right. We are called to reach out to others. On rare occasions that can happen on a grand scale. But most of the time it happens in simple acts of kindness of one person to another. . . . There

in that strange place for just that one
moment, I was in harmony with God's
will, bonded together with this young man
in a most unlikely but marvelous way.[60]

Yes, God's will and our passion generally go
hand in hand to make a difference in the lives of
those around us—or around the world. What we
do with our talents can affect others for eternity,
for as Dr. Joe Stowell says, "People are the only
eternal commodities; everything else will be
held at the border."[61] God glories in the beauty
of seeing you enjoying the talents He gifted you
with. Don't waste your precious life, dear sister!
Make it count for something that lasts.

| *Cry* from my **Heart** | *I'm searching my heart, Lord, to see exactly what I have a passion for. I'm determined to use that passion for You and those You want me to impact.* |

100 Percent

"We love him," wrote the Apostle John, "because he first loved us (1 John 4:19 KJV). God took the first step toward us, showing His love for us in a most dramatic way as He sent Jesus to earth to die in our place. What an amazing truth! You'd think our natural reaction would be to fall at His feet and love Him back, willing to do *anything* for Him as a "thank You" for all He has done. Yet when you think about it, sometimes it's embarrassing how shallow our love is in comparison to His. I, for one, still struggle with wanting to maintain control in my life. A constant prayer of mine is "Not my will but Yours be done," because my will asserts itself every day.

Back in the 1800s, Jonathan Goforth was serving as a minister with no thought of ever being a missionary; in fact, he rejected the idea.

Then he heard Dr. G. L. Mackay, a pioneer missionary to Taiwan, tell of how he had been unable to persuade anyone to come to Taiwan (then Formosa) to help him. Goforth said,

> As I listened to these words, I was overcome with shame. . . . There was I, bought with the precious blood of Jesus Christ, daring to dispose of my life as I pleased. . . . From that hour I became a foreign missionary.[62]

Goforth spent forty-six years as a missionary in China, leading some thirteen thousand to faith in Christ.

So we should all become missionaries, right? No, that's not the point. The key point in what Goforth said is that phrase "*daring to dispose of my life as I pleased.*" Who makes the moment-by-moment decisions in our lives—us or God? Most of us are happy to give God the control over certain parts of our lives, but we struggle with giving Him total control. In fact, I think control is the big issue for most of us in committing our lives totally to God.

One of the reasons we hold back giving 100 percent to God is because our perspective is so small. We think that if we do turn over control to Him, we'll miss out on the fun in life. We're wearing blinders that keep us from seeing the big picture of what the Christian life is meant to be. There are joys out there that we have not yet experienced because we're holding back on total commitment to God. C. S. Lewis said, "We are half-hearted creatures, fooling about with drink and sex and ambition when infinite joy is offered us, like an ignorant child who wants to go on making mud pies in a slum because he cannot imagine what is meant by the offer of a holiday at the sea. We are far too easily pleased."[63]

For a moment, let's talk motivation. What should be the motivating factor that causes us to turn over our lives 100 percent to God?

* Guilt? *My sins are so bad that I owe it to God to live for Him.*

* Duty? *After the sacrifice He has made for me, I really should live my life completely for Him.*

* Fear? *If I don't live totally for Him, He'll make life hard for me, and I'll be miserable.*

No, no, no! Whatever we do for God should be done out of love for Him and in response to His love for us. Do you remember we started out with that verse, "We love him, because he first loved us" (1 John 4:19)? He wants a love relationship with us. The very first directive He gave us was to "love the LORD your God with all your heart and with all your soul and with all your strength" (Deuteronomy 6:5). There's not much we can give to the God who owns everything. But one thing we can give Him is our love.

Francis Chan calls it "crazy love"—living for God, not just because we made a commitment to Him, but because we love Him with every fiber of our being. Our relationship is that close. He said His connection with us is like that of a husband who is crazy-in-love with his bride. And His heart longs for our love in return. Not a puny "I- like-you-and-you-like-me" liaison but a fervent passion.

Our relationship with God will never bring joy to His heart if it's with the idea of "How little can I give God and get away with it?" He wants us to live for Him 100 percent because He died for us 100 percent.

God is wildly in love with us. How do we describe our love for Him? Is my love based on how God performs, whether He gives me what I ask for? As Francis Chan asks, "Are we in love with God or just His stuff? Do I serve God because I promised I would? Or do I serve Him because I'm passionately in love with Him?"[64]

John Piper wrote, "I am constantly astonished at people who say they believe in God but live as though happiness were to be found by giving Him two percent of their attention."[65] Do we think God is pleased if we manage to fit Him into our lives in some small way? Is He content with leftovers—leftover time, leftover energy? Famous preacher G. Campbell Morgan talked about "sacrilege," a word we don't use very often any more. He said, "Sacrilege is often defined as taking something that belongs to God and using it profanely. But there is a bigger sacrilege we commit all the time. That is to take something and give it to God when it means absolutely nothing to us."[66] What you give to God—is it valuable to you, or just leftovers?

You and I are more precious than diamonds to God. Pour out your love to Him who purchased your relationship with Him "not with perishable things such as silver or gold . . . but with the precious blood of Christ" (1 Peter 1:18–19).

Cry **from my Heart** | *Not my will, Lord, but Yours—every moment of today—because I love You.*

God.

You are relentless.
I have yielded
Everything to You—
Everything but one small exception—
An exception so small
I'm truly amazed
You would even take notice.
Yet it is invariably
To that one small exception
That You keep bringing me
Back, and back, and back.
Why does it matter so much to You?

My child,

Why does it matter so much to you?

– Ruth Harms Calkin
The One Year Book of Bible Promises[67]

Never Give Up!

"Do you want me to tell you about the greatest athlete I've ever seen?" asked Peter Ueberroth when he was speaking to the Empire Club in Toronto, Canada. Ueberroth is the man who very successfully headed the 1984 Summer Olympics in Los Angeles. Whereas previous Olympics had ended with large deficits, the 1984 Olympics is considered the most financially successful in history. After that accomplishment, for a number of years Ueberroth was the commissioner of US Major League Baseball. Now when you think about a man who has had as much exposure to sports as Ueberroth, you know that every ear perked up when he asked this question.

He said that in the 1984 Olympics, they had a twenty-thousand-kilometer torch run winding all the way through the US. The Torch Relay was an idea that originated with his Olympic Committee. Each runner would light his torch from that of the previous runner, run one kilo-meter, and light the torch of the next runner.

Peter said that he got the films of the torch run every day from the three television networks, and at about 9:00 p.m. he would look at the film from the day before. Early one morning his staff came into his office and said, "We want you to see a film on the torch." Peter tells about it in his own words:

> I said I had seen it the night before, but they said this was a private one and insisted that I look at it. When they stuck it in the player, I saw it was a little piece of amateur video. It showed a nine-year-old girl bent over, severely handicapped, holding on to a torch with both hands, waiting for the next runner from behind to come up.
>
> The camera panned down the road and there was a runner with a full stride, carrying the Olympic flame in his torch. He came and he lit her torch and it took him awhile because she was obviously very handicapped. Up came a motorcycle policeman—a heavy guy with one of those big aerospace plastic things in front of his face—and he was unhappy and gunning the engines at

this delay. And I was wondering, why am I seeing this film?

Then this little youngster started, and took a step and slowly but surely she started . . . her kilometer. I noticed it was a little uphill. I was later told that she could not walk on flat land; she had to walk against the gravity. She picked up speed. And then I saw the reason they had the film for me—because when her head came up, her smile was as big as this whole room! From one ear to the other! And she kept running, and she kept running—step by step by step. And then I noticed people were about eight deep on both sides in this little town in New Mexico. They were waving flags, cheering, all carrying flags saying, "RUN, AMY, RUN." She kept running. . . . Somehow her smile got bigger and bigger and she was wringing wet and she kept going until she finished the kilometer. She made it! She lit the next torch and the runner was off on the dash.

The cheers were virtually deafening for this little youngster who was so proud—such a great moment for her. Just before the film ended, the cameraman turned to the motorcycle policeman who was on the side of the road with his plastic thing up—and a handkerchief out wiping his eyes.[68]

See, that's really what life is all about. We run as hard as we can, carrying the torch of Jesus Christ. Sometimes we don't want to go on. Sometimes we want to drop it and quit. But we're here to say to one another in this life, "Run, Amy, run. Run, Pearl, run. Run, Gina, run!" Don't give up!

The author of Hebrews says, "Let us run with perseverance the race marked out for us" (12:1). In the Christian life, however, don't think that everybody is in one enormous competition, trying to outdo each other. That's not what the writer of Hebrews had in mind. No, the Christian life is an endurance race where each of us is challenged individually to finish the course.

Moreover, it is a race "marked out for us," a race that is unique for each one of us, a race designed for us by God Himself.

For some of us, the race is long—a marathon. I have a friend who runs marathons two or three times a year. But though 26.2 miles seems to me to be a very long race, it is far from the longest race in the world—the Self-Transcendence Marathon, which is 3,100 miles long and lasts fifty-two days. The idea is to test the runners to discover the limits of their endurance and try to go beyond them. God may see fit to leave you on this earth for eighty, ninety, or one hundred years or more. Yours is a race that is long and hard.

For others, the race is a one-hundred-meter sprint, a race where we give our best but where the time of our race is short. Oswald Chambers, who wrote the famous devotional book *My Utmost for His Highest,* was a missionary to Egypt after World War I. He died at the young age of thirty-three, yet his writings have touched the lives of countless thousands. Jim Elliot, one of the five missionaries who was speared to death by the Huaoranis in Ecuador in the 1950s, was only twenty-nine when he died. Yet he will be long remembered for saying, "He is no fool who gives what he cannot keep to gain that which he cannot lose."

For others of us, the race of life is a walk-a-thon, for we are the plodders who day after day keep putting one foot in front of the other. We don't get our names in the headlines or on a news feed. But we faithfully keep going until we reach the end of our race. What does God say to us at the end of our walk-a-thon? "Well done, good and faithful servant! You have been faithful with a few things; I will put you in charge of many things. Come and share your master's happiness!" (Matthew 25:23). No words of reproof because we didn't run faster or longer. Just commendation for faithfulness.

Then there are hurdles, a race with barriers that must be crossed during the course. No doubt you know someone whose life seems to be a series of hurdles. They hardly make it over one major problem before being confronted by another.

I have friends, Jim and Edna, who were missionaries in Colombia for a number of years. They know what it is to run the hurdles in life. To start with, Edna is blind in one eye. On top of that, she is not the thrill-seeking type, so missionary life in some remote area was not on her bucket list. During their first one and a half years in Colombia, two miscarriages, surgery to remove an ovary, and a pregnancy took their toll on her body, though she was thrilled at the birth of their precious Heather Lynn. Her husband's job as a pilot providing transportation for missionaries in the jungle areas required that he be gone a good deal. When he *was* home, he was exhausted. Then a FARC guerilla uprising and

kidnapping on their base forced them to evacu-
ate and move to Bogotá. Shortly afterwards,
the little police station in front of the Bogotá
guesthouse complex was blown up by a bomb.
Then just before they were to return to the US
for furlough, Jim had a massive stroke requiring
life-risking emergency surgery and leaving him
in need of long and extensive physical therapy
in the US.

To make a long story shorter, after Jim's
recuperation and their return to missions in
Colombia, they learned that their only child,
Heather, who had graduated from Wheaton
College and was living in the US, had developed acute myelogenous leukemia. Edna flew
home to care for her, but in a matter of months,
they lost her. Six months later they were on a
new assignment—in the Philippines, and that's
where I met Edna.

One hurdle after another had confronted
her. Edna said, "The tears still come, sometimes at unexpected times. After all, we experienced an amputation. But by God's grace, we
are living life in a new way with God's peace.
A verse that means a lot to me is 1 Corinthians
15:58—'Therefore, my beloved brethren, be
ye steadfast, unmovable, always abounding in

the work of the Lord, forasmuch as ye know that your labour is not in vain in the Lord'" (KJV). God bless you, Edna. You are clearing the hurdles one at a time—an example to the rest of us who are running.

Let me encourage you: You can run the race God lays out for you because it is deliberately planned and uniquely suited for you. It's neither too long nor too difficult. God knows your strengths and weaknesses, your abilities and inabilities, and He takes these into account as He lays out your course.

God gave you life when half a million sperm competed to fertilize one egg that became you. (How's that for being popular!) You are an original. Psalm 139 tells us that God literally knit you in your mother's womb. You may wish you were like someone else, but you are the person God wants to have a relationship with.

In *Created for a Purpose*, I tell about Richard Clem, who bought an old pickle bottle at a yard sale—an amber-colored, eleven-inch-tall bottle. He paid three dollars for it. When he realized it was probably quite old, he offered it for sale on eBay. Much to his surprise, after only one week and sixty bids, his three-dollar pickle bottle sold for $44,100!

Some mornings, do you wake up feeling worth about as much as a three-dollar pickle bottle? You feel old, tired, almost worthless—about all you're good for is to sit on a shelf. Your struggle with a wrong sense of self-worth may show up as an eating disorder, compulsive behavior, addiction, depression, or fearfulness. You hesitate to step out for God.

Take heart! You're worth far more than $44,100! God was willing to pay for you with the death of His only Son. You're priceless!

Paul put it in perspective in Philippians 3:13–14: "Forgetting what is behind and straining toward what is ahead, I press on toward the goal to win the prize for which God has called me heavenward in Christ Jesus."

We have been given a race to run. Remember that the writer of Hebrews tells us we're to run the race with *perseverance*? And how do we do that? The secret is in Hebrews 12:2: "looking to Jesus, the pioneer and perfecter of our faith." It's when we take our eyes off Him that we get offtrack and want to quit.

What takes my eyes off Jesus? I made a list:

●   Busyness—thinking I can get along
     without time in the Word and prayer

* My focus—when the mountain in front of me becomes bigger than God

* Carelessness—being distracted by responsibilities, even a misplaced desire for entertainment and hobbies. Luke sums this one up as "cares and riches and pleasures of this life" (Luke 8:14 NLT).

One of the great moments of sports history took place on August 7, 1954, when the only two men who had ever broken the four-minute mile met in a race at the 1954 British Empire and Commonwealth Games hosted in Vancouver, British Columbia. In May of that same year Roger Bannister had been the first to break the then-thought-impossible four-minute mile with a time of 3:59.4. A month later, John Landy ran the mile in 3:57.9. Now for the first time, the two would be competing in the "Race of the Century." John Landy was leading until the final turn on the last lap, when he glanced over his left shoulder, allowing Bannister to pass him on the right. When Landy took his eyes off the goal and looked to see what his competition was doing, that was all that was necessary for Bannister to surge around him and win the race.[69]

Fix your eyes on Jesus and don't look back. Embrace the race of life as designed for you by God Himself. Consider what God has allowed in your life to be part of His plan for you. You were created for a purpose. Strive to take hold of that purpose for which He has taken hold of you (Philippians 3:12). That race God has given you—run! Don't give up!

❂ ❂ ❂

On March 3, 2011, eleven-year-old Jessica Joy Reese was diagnosed with an inoperable and incurable brain tumor. Jessica began her treatment consisting of thirty rounds of radiation and daily chemotherapy. While at the children's hospital where she was being treated, she saw all the other children fighting various cancers. "How can we help them?" she asked her parents. She wanted to do something! And so Jessica developed a little motto: **"NEGU,"** which stands for "Never Ever Give Up," and invented "JoyJars," jars filled with new toys and activities for ill children. Jessica lost her fight with cancer but she never gave up—she started a global movement of compassion that has now reached eighty thousand children fighting cancer in twenty-seven countries.

So, don't *you* dare give up! Don't settle for running half a kilometer. Say, "God, You created me for a purpose. I'm going to take hold of that purpose You have for me."

Yes, you are more precious than diamonds. You can be exactly what God created you to be. Never, ever give up!

Cry
from
my
Heart

Dear Lord, help me to run my race today with my eyes on You. And to never, ever give up!

who would you be,

what would you do,

if you weren't afraid?

Acknowledgments

"Are you writing another book?"
I'm often asked. For a long time I've
answered, "No, right now I'm just 'taking
in' so I'll possibly have something to give
out in the future—in God's time." But then Paul
Muckley, former Senior Editor for Non-Fiction
at Barbour Publishing, proposed a title, *More
Precious Than Diamonds*, that set me to thinking. And this little volume is the outcome.

Of course, it is reaching you only with the
help of many others. Once again, my daughter
Bonnie has contributed so much—not only of
her writing skills but her life insights as well,
learned through pain-filled times of personal
crisis. Women have freely shared their some-
times-heartrending life experiences to help other
women grasp that God uses tough tools, if
necessary, to cut and polish us into His beautiful
jewels. My neighbor and friend Terri Van
Workum meticulously looked up every Scripture reference to be sure each one was quoted
correctly. And my husband, author of sixty-five

books himself, took time to contribute his experienced advice.

Anyone who writes owes a debt of gratitude to her editors. Barbour Publications' former editorial coordinator, Amy Oakley, and copyeditor Jill Jones have both helped me cut out the superfluous and keep the best. Karen Huang has been a "jewel" to make sure details are correct and has been a delight to work with, along with Stef Juan, the back-up editor. Typesetter Aileen Barrongo and cover artist Amor Aurelio Alvarez have worked behind the scenes to provide the right setting. A big thanks to all of you for using your God-given skills.

May Jesus Christ be praised!

Notes

1   J. Courtney Sullivan, "How Diamonds Became
    Forever," published: May 3, 2013 *New York Times*,
    Weddings/Celebrations, http://www.nytimes.com/2013/05/05/
    fashion/weddings/how-americans-learned-to-love-diamonds.
    html?pagewanted=2, accessed 4-18-14.

2   "Golkonda," http://en.wikipedia.org/wiki/Golkonda, accessed
    3-12-14.

3   John F. Burns, "New Delhi Journal: Crown Jewels of the
    Nizam: All Are India's Now," *The New York Times*,
    February 2, 1995, http://www.nytimes.com/1995/02/02/world/
    new-delhi-journal-crown-jewels-of-the-nizam-all-are-india-s-now.html,
    accessed 3-12-14.

4   "Osman Ali Khan Asaf Jah VII," http://en.wikipedia.org/wiki/
    Osman_Ali_Khan,_Asaf_Jah_VII, accessed 3-12-14.

5   Alexandra Sifferlin, "Bill Gates Is The Richest Man in the
    World (Again)," *Time*, March 3, 2014, http://time.com/11389/
    bill-gates-worlds-richest-man/, accessed 3-12-14.

6   Burns, "New Delhi Journal," *The New York Times*, accessed
    3-12-14.

7   Anika Mohla, "From richest to rags in seven generations,"
    October 21, 2012, http://newindianexpress.com/magazine/
    article1306390.ece#.UxydR152ceM/, accessed 3-12-14.

8   "Osman Ali Khan Asaf Jah VII," *Wikipedia*, accessed
    3-12-14.

9   Robert Frank, "Most expensive diamond ever sold goes for
    $83.2M," http://www.cnbc.com/id/101196278/ . November 13, 2013,
    accessed 3-12-14.

10 "What Is the Most Valuable Diamond?" http://wiki.answers.
    com/
    Q/What_is_the_most_valuable_diamond,n.d., accessed 3-12-14.

11 Jeffrey Post (curator of the Smithsonian National Gem and
    Mineral Collection and diamond expert), "Diamonds
    Unearthed," http://www.smithsonianmag.com/science-nature/
    diamonds-unearthed-141629226/?c=y%3Fno-ist, accessed 3-12-14.

12 David Eckman, *Becoming Who God Intended* (Eugene, OR: Harvest House Publishers, 2005), 24.

13 Alice Arenas, "Social Media True Confessions," Alice Arenas Blog, *Social Media for Business*, October 29, 2013, http://saneracamp.com/2012/10/social-media-self-esteem-true-confessions/, accessed 3-12-14.

14 Ann Voskamp, "How the Hidden Dangers of Comparison are Killing Us . . . (and Our Daughters)": The Measuring Stick Principle, *A Holy Experience*, November 6, 2013, http://www.aholyexperience.com/?s=How+the+Hidden+Dangers+of+Comparison+are+Killing+Us, accessed 3-12-14.

15 "Marilyn's Quest for Love," United Press International, *The Dispatch*, Lexington, NC: November 14, 1960, 5.

16 "Marilyn Monroe," last modified March 8, 2014, http://en.wikipedia.org/wiki/Marilyn_Monroe, accessed 3-12-2014.

17 Brent Curtis & John Eldredge, *The Sacred Romance* (Nashville, TN: Thomas Nelson, 1997), 164.

18 Kimberly D. Henderson, "For When You Want to Freak Out Because You Just Keep Getting Older," *A Planting of the Lord*, April 29, http://aplantingofthelord.com/2014/04/what-my-husband-really-needs-for-when-you-just-want-to-freak-out-because-you-just-keep-getting-older.html, accessed June 4, 2014.

19 John Lincoln, "The Discovery and History of the Cullinan Diamond," https://www.youtube.com/channel/UCAX_FqnUiSdKWB-nPt2aUTqg, accessed 6-9-14.

20 "The Cullinan," Famous Diamonds, Historic Royal Palaces, Tower of London, http://www.hrp.org.uk/toweroflondon/stories/palacehighlights/crownjewels/otherjewels, accessed 6-9-14.

21 "Diamond Cutting," *Wikipedia*, file:///Users/dssmac/Desktop/CULLINAN&CUTTING/Diamond%20cutting%20-%20Wikipedia,%20the%20free%20encyclopedia.html, accessed 4-9-14.

22 "Cutting The Cullinan" by Forevermark, https://www.youtube.com/watch?v=2NKebH-wg-M, accessed 6-9-14.

23 Mrs. Charles E. Cowman, *Streams in the Desert* (Grand Rapids, MI: Daybreak Books, 1995), 129.

24 "The Cullinan Diamond," Royal Collection Trust, http://www.royalcollection.org.uk/exhibitions/diamonds-a-jubilee-celebration/the-cullinan-diamond, accessed 6-8-14.

25   Michael Savage, "The Big Question: What makes diamonds valuable, and why do we revere them so much?", *The Independent*, Tuesday, September 23, 2008, http://www. independent.co.uk/news/science/the-big-question-what-makes-diamonds-valuable-and-why-do-we-revere-them-so-much-938879.html, accessed 6-7-14.

26   Charles Spurgeon, *Beside Still Waters* (Nashville, TN: Thomas Nelson, 1999), 28.

27   The story of Karin and David is used with their permission.

28   The story of Bernadette and Alex is used with their permission.

29   "Diamond Cutting," *Wikipedia*, accessed 4-9-14.

30   "Diamond Cut," *Wikipedia*, http://en.wikipedia.org/wiki/ Diamond_cut, accessed 6-9-14.

31   Thomas Carlyle, http://www.brainyquote.com/quotes/quotes/t/ thomascarl120684.html, accessed 6-20-14.

32   Madame Guyon, *Experiencing the Depths of Jesus Christ* (Sargent, GA: Christian Books Publishing House, n.d.), 131.

33   Dr. Jack W. Hayford, *The Mary Miracle* (Ventura: Regal, 1994), 99.

34   Mary Stevenson, "Footprints in the Sand", http://www. footprints-inthe-sand.com/index.php?page=Poem/Poem.php, accessed 3-13-14.

35   Dr. Jerry Bergman, "The Earth: Unique in All the Universe," *Insight* (March 1980), http://creationsd.org/PDF-insight-articles/ The_Earth_Is_Unique_In_All_The_Universe.pdf, accessed 4-11-14.

36   Corrie ten Boom, *Each New Day*, "He Can Handle It," May 28/Worry (Grand Rapids, MI: Revell, a division of Baker Publishing Group, 1977, 2003), 95.

37   Richard Foster, *Freedom of Simplicity* (Aylesbury, Bucks, UK: Hazell, Watson & Viney Ltd., 1981), 114-115.

38   Ibid.

39   Ann Voskamp, *One Thousand Gifts* (Grand Rapids, MI: Zondervan, 2010), 12.

40   Ibid.

41   Kim Thomas, *Even God Rested* (Eugene, OR: Harvest House Publishers, 2003), 72.

42   Cynthia Heald, *A Woman's Journey to the Heart of God* (Nashville, TN: Thomas Nelson, 1997), 25-26.

43   Ibid., 207.

44   Jill Briscoe, *The Garden of Grace* (Oxford, England: Monarch Books, a publishing imprint of Lion Hudson, 2007), 11.

45   Joseph M. Stowell, *Coming Home* (Chicago: Moody Press, 1998), 87.

46   Jill Briscoe, *The Garden of Grace*, 110-112.

47   Ibid.

48   Elisabeth Elliott, "Why is God Doing This to Me?" The Elisabeth Elliot Newsletter, January/February 1988, http://www.elisabethelliot.org/newsletters2/jan.feb.1988.pdf, accessed 3-14-14.

49   Bruce Wilkinson, *Secrets of the Vine Devotional* (Sisters, OR: Multnomah Publishers, Inc., 2002), 86.

50   Charles R. Swindoll, *So You Want to Be Like Christ? Eight Essentials to Get You There,* Christian Book Summaries, Volume 3, Issue 38, September 2007.

51   C. S. Lewis, "The Seeing Eye," in *Lewis: Christian Reflections,* ed. Walter Hooper (Grand Rapids, MI: Eerdmans, 1975), 168-169.

52   W. E. Vine, *Vine's Expository Dictionary of New Testament Words,* Unabridged Edition (McLean, VA: MacDonald Publishing Company, n.d.), 924.

53   Guyon, *Experiencing the Depths of Jesus Christ,* 32.

54   Ruth Myers, *The Satisfied Heart* (Colorado Springs, CO: WaterBrook Press, 1999), 48.

55   Ruth Harms Calkin, *The One Year Book of Bible Promises* (Wheaton, IL: Tyndale House Publishers Inc., 2000), October 10 entry.

56   Mary M. Byers, *How to Say No and Live to Tell About It* (Eugene, OR: Harvest House Publishers, 2006), 113.

57   Dr. Margaret E. Brand with Dr. James L. Jost, *Vision for God* (Grand Rapids, MI: Discovery House Publishers, 2006), 111-112.

58   Byers, *How to Say No and Live to Tell About It*, 37.

59   Francis S. Collins, *The Language of God* (New York: Free Press, 2008), 213-217.

60   Ibid.

61   Dr. Joseph M. Stowell, *Following Christ* (Grand Rapids, MI: Zondervan Publishing House, 1966), 116.

62   Rosalind Goforth, *Goforth of China* (from the chapter entitled "Early Leadings"), Evangelical Revival Series, No. 153, The Revival Library, Kindle edition, http://www.amazon.com/Goforth-Of-China-Rosalind/dp/1163138959#reader_B00H6Q1Q8G, accessed 12-21-2014.

63   C. S. Lewis, *The Weight of Glory and Other Addresses*, https://www.goodreads.com/quotes/702-it-would-seem-that-our-lord-finds-our-desires-not, accessed 4-3-2014.

64   Francis Chan, *Crazy Love* (Colorado Springs, CO: David C. Cook, 2008), 62.

65   John Piper, *Desiring God* (Portland, OR: Multnomah Press, 1986), 240.

66   G. Campbell Morgan, as quoted by Ravi Zacharias with R. S. B. Sawyer, *Walking from East to West* (Grand Rapids; MI: Zondervan, 2006), 68.

67   Calkin, *The One Year Book of Bible Promises*, August 26 entry.

68   http://speeches.empireclub.org/61516/data, The Empire Club of Canada Addresses (Toronto, Canada), April 24, 1985, 455-474, accessed May 9, 2013.

69   "John Landy," http://en.wikipedia.org/wiki/John_Landy, accessed 4-21-14.

About the Author

DARLENE SALA, along with her husband, Harold, is co-founder of Guidelines International Ministries, which reaches into more than 100 countries of the world. She has had an active ministry role as pastor's wife, mentor, Bible teacher, and missionary. An international conference speaker, Darlene has authored eleven books and produces a two-minute weekly radio program called "Encouraging Words." She is the mother of three adult children, and grandmother of eight.

If this book has been an encouragement and help to you, Darlene would like to hear from you.

Write to her at:
info@guidelines.org

Guidelines International Ministries
26161 Marguerite Parkway, Suite F
Mission Viejo, CA 92692
Tel 949.582.5001

Visit us at:
www.guidelines.org

Join us online at:

 Facebook.com/Guidelines International Ministries

 Twitter.com/guidelinesintl

Youtube.com/c/GuidelinesOrgVideos

Subscribe to Darlene's *Encouraging Words* weekly e-mail by sending an e-mail to:
encouragingwords@guidelines.org

We would love
to hear from you!

Please share with us
how this book has helped or blessed you.

You can send your comments and suggestions
through any of the following channels

Call us: +63(2) 531-4303
Email us: inquire@omflit.com
Buy from us: +639159191262
              estore@omflit.com
              www.passages.com.ph

You may also join our online conversation:

Facebook.com/omfliterature

Twitter.com/omflit

Youtube.com/omflit

Instagram.com/omfliterature

Pinterest.com/omflit

Subscribe to our e-newsletter by sending an email to:
newchapters@omflit.com

www.OMFLit.com

OMF LITERATURE INC.
Publishing Truth.
Shaping Generations.
www.OMFLit.com